Arrivals

How long can
a secret be kept?

Brian Gallagher

THE O'BRIEN PRESS
DUBLIN

First published 2016 by The O'Brien Press Ltd,
12 Terenure Road East, Rathgar, Dublin 6, D06 HD27, Ireland.
Tel: +353 1 4923333; Fax: +353 1 4922777
E-mail: books@obrien.ie
Website: www.obrien.ie
The O'Brien Press is a member of Publishing Ireland.

ISBN: 978-1-84717-720-9

8 7 6 5 4 3 2 1
20 19 18 17 16

Printed and bound by CPI Group (UK) Ltd, Croydon, CR0 4YY.

The paper in this book is produced using pulp from managed forests.

Published in:

DUBLIN
UNESCO
City of Literature

DEDICATION

To Eileen and Lorne – thanks for all the years of friendship.

ACKNOWLEDGEMENTS

My sincere thanks to Michael O'Brien for supporting the idea of a novel dealing with Irish emigration to Canada, to my editor, Marian Broderick, for her editing and advice, to publicists Ruth Heneghan, Geraldine Feehily, and Carol Hurley for all their efforts on my behalf, to Emma Byrne for her excellent work on cover design, and to everyone at The O'Brien Press, with whom, as ever, it's a pleasure to work.

My thanks also go to Hugh McCusker for his painstaking proofreading, and I'm grateful to Denis Courtney for his support, and to Zoe O'Brien, Harry Webster, Eva Cunningham and Jillian Jones, four young readers who shared with me their views of an early draft of the story.

A huge vote of thanks goes to Eileen Nolan and Lorne Kelsey for providing the initial spark that led to the writing of *Arrivals*, for the warmth of their hospitality, and for always managing to point me in the right direction during my Canadian research.

For information on Ojibwe culture I am indebted to Murray and Dan Whetung, and especially to Anne Taylor, Archivist at Curve Lake Cultural Centre.

At Lakefield College former Dean John Boyko went out of his way to be helpful, as did Tracey Blodgett, who unearthed vital information from the school records.

During research in Northern Ireland I was extended every courtesy and assistance by Catherine McCullough, Head of Learning, Ulster Folk Park, Dr Brian Lambkin, Mellon Centre for Migration, Dr Patrick Fitzgerald, National Museum of Northern Ireland and Dr Joanne Devlin Trew, University of Ulster.

The expertise of all of the above was freely shared with me, but any errors, or opinions expressed, are mine and mine alone.

And finally, no amount of thanks could express my gratitude for the constant support and encouragement of my family, Miriam, Orla and Peter.

Prologue

July 2nd 1928
Lake Katchewanooka,
Ontario, Canada

Lucy stayed absolutely still, knowing her life was in danger. Her heart pounded, but she concentrated on not making the slightest sound. Instead she squatted behind a stack of wooden crates in the deep shadows at the back of the boathouse.

It was a beautiful day outside, with sunlight glinting on the surface of the lake, but it was shady here in the old wooden boathouse. Despite the reedy, damp air, Lucy could feel a trickle of perspiration at the back of her neck. She wanted to wipe it away, but she forced herself not to move, and stayed crouched on the floor, her hands clasped around her knees to stop them from knocking together.

She listened to the two men who had entered the boathouse.

The bigger man, Brent Packham, was a wealthy businessman who was rumoured to be involved with running whiskey and rum across the Canadian border into America, where selling alcohol was still illegal. Smuggling liquor was a trade that involved gangsters, and Lucy had thought it would be exciting to sneak into the grounds and do a little snooping on the lakeside estate that Brent Packham had rented for the summer. She had thought that her friends Will and Mike would be impressed with her daring. But now she was terrified she was going to witness a murder.

The house and grounds were north of the town of Lakefield, on the upper corner of Lake Katchewanooka, near where Lucy and her mother lived on the Otonabee Reserve with other members of the Ojibwe tribe. The thought of her mother made Lucy wish she was home now. But there was no use longing for the security of being with Mom – she had got herself into this fix and she would have to get herself out again.

Now that she was twelve, Lucy had been given the freedom to explore the nearby lakes in her canoe, while painting and sketching. It was how she had met Will and Mike – though she hadn't told Mom about making friends with boys who didn't live on the reserve.

This afternoon she had been following the trail along the wooded shoreline when she almost stumbled onto the two men. Their voices alerted her just in time, and she ran into the rambling old wooden boathouse. Unfortunately the men stopped at the door.

'Let's step inside,' said Brent Packham.

Lucy ducked down behind a pile of wooden boxes and held her breath.

'We won't be disturbed here,' said Packham, entering the boathouse.

Lucy peeked out. She was frightened of being found, but also curious about what was going on. Mr Packham was said to have a shady past, but he owned a brewery and a transport company in the nearby city of Peterborough. He was a big, muscular man with oiled black hair. And although he dressed in fine clothes – almost to the point of looking like a dandy – there was still an air of threat about him, the sense of someone that it would be foolish to cross. The other man was slighter and less prosperous-looking.

'I'm glad you came to see me, Jake,' Packham said. 'Always better to iron out problems man to man.'

'That's what I think too.'

'So?'

'So, I think we should renegotiate. Each month we're shifting more whiskey over the border, Mister P – making you a fortune.'

So he *was* a smuggler, thought Lucy.

'I'm running a profitable business,' said Packham, his tone reasonable. 'And you're sharing those profits.'

'Not sharing them enough.'

'I say it is enough.'

'And I say it's not.'

Lucy listened intently, intrigued despite her nervousness.

'Then don't work for me,' said Packham, his voice taking on a hard edge. 'The Verelli family are eager to expand – I can go to them.'

'*I'm* your American partner. Using someone else…that would bring problems…'

'So now you're threatening me, Jake,' said Packham, and Lucy knew instinctively that, despite Packham's controlled tone, the man called Jake was living dangerously.

'Just stating the facts,' he said.

'Let me state a fact,' said Packham.

Lucy heard a quick rustle of clothes, then a sharp intake of breath.

'This is a Colt Forty-Five,' said Packham, 'and I've used it before. How do you like *that* fact?'

Lucy bit her lip in fear. On the reserve people hunted for food with rifles, but Lucy knew what a Colt pistol was, and the kind of damage it could do at close range.

'Please, Brent!' cried Jake. 'I was just…I was just negotiating!'

'Really? Sounded like you were threatening my business.'

'It wasn't personal, Brent, I swear! It was just…just dealing!'

'Threaten my business and you threaten me. I can't have it out there that Brent Packham was threatened.'

'No, Brent, please, we can work this out! No-one needs to know!'

'But *I'd* know, Jake. And *you'd* know. You'd know you threatened me and got away with it. I can't have that.'

Lucy felt her heart pounding as though it were going to explode. She thought of the words of her pastor, who said all it took for bad things to happen, was for good people to do nothing. And if she did nothing Brent Packham was going to kill another man! But if she stepped out of her hiding place and pleaded for Jake's life what would happen then? A man who was willing to shoot his business partner – even if that partner was a gangster – might have no qualms about killing her as a witness. Especially as she was a trespasser, and from the Ojibwe Reserve.

'I'm sorry I offended you, Brent,' pleaded Jake. 'but we can fix this. I see your point. I understand that I have to pay a price, so how's this? Instead of increasing my share, I drop my price. As a peace offering I drop my share by ten percent for the rest of this year? What do you say, Brent?'

Say yes, thought Lucy. Please, say yes!

There was a pause, then Packham spoke. 'I don't think so, Jake. Threatening me was stupid and greedy. Worst of all it was a betrayal. Bad move. *Fatal* move.'

'Please, Brent! I'm sorry! We'll make it twenty – no, twenty-five percent less! You'll never get a deal like that from the Verelli family. What do you say, Brent, twenty-five percent of a saving, and I swear I'll never let you down again!'

Lucy heard a trigger being cocked. Despite all her efforts to remain still, she flinched at the sound. To her horror she realised that she had pushed backwards against the boathouse wall, which creaked. It wasn't a loud sound, but had Packham heard it? Lucy looked around in panic. There was a door in the rear wall of the boathouse. If she got it open now, maybe she could get out the back before Packham got to her. Or would that be suicidal, with Packham likely to shoot her in the back, as she tried to run away?

Time seemed to stand still and she struggled to control her panic. She looked at the door, five or six feet away, and listened intently to hear if Packham was coming. She tried to still her mind and think clearly. Run and maybe escape? But also maybe get shot. Or stay and risk discovery – but maybe get away with it?

Suddenly the decision was made for her, as Packham spoke, and Lucy realised that his attention was still focussed on Jake.

'You were a two-bit hoodlum when I met you,' said Packham. 'I gave you your break, and you stab me in the back. No loyalty. In your heart of hearts, you're still a two-bit hoodlum.'

'No, Brent.'

'Yes, Brent!' cried Packham, his voice raised now. 'You're not worth a bullet – I won't waste one on you.'

Packham had raised his voice in anger for the first time, yet despite cocking the pistol he was now saying that he wouldn't shoot. Had he just wanted to terrify Jake to teach him a lesson? Lucy prayed this was the case and that the two men would leave the boathouse alive. But part of her felt that that was too good to be true. Maybe Packham was lying about not wasting a bullet, maybe he was playing cat and mouse with his victim while intending to shoot him in the end.

Before Lucy could agonise any further there was a flurry of movement and the sound of a sickening blow, immediately followed by a cry from Jake. Lucy heard him slump, moaning, to the ground, then came the awful sound of three more heavy blows in swift succession, after which Jake moaned no further.

Lucy remained completely still, crouched in the gloom of the boathouse, horrified by what she had heard, and terrified of being discovered.

Part One

Introductions

CHAPTER ONE

Terminal Two, Dublin Airport

April 2015

Ciara loved a mystery. Her nineteen-year-old brother Connor had affectionately nicknamed her Sherlock, and her favourite books were crime stories in which someone had to unravel a mystery. Ciara's sister, Sarah, who was seventeen, and who thought she was too advanced now for stories like that, had given Ciara all of her Nancy Drew and Anthony Horowitz books – which Ciara had devoured.

However, it was one thing to read about a mystery, another thing altogether to solve one in real life. But that was what Ciara hoped to do. She sat with her father in the coffee dock opposite their departure gate, sipping a smoothie and savouring the novelty of preparing to cross the Atlantic on a special trip.

She was enjoying the smoothie's sweetness as she took in her surroundings. She loved the airport and its futuristic terminal building. With its blue lights, soaring escalators, and gleaming glass and steel, it seemed to Ciara like a space station. She liked the hustle and bustle as passengers prepared to fly all over the world.

'Excited?' asked Dad now as he put down his coffee cup, smiling.

'Yeah, can't wait to get there.'

'Enjoy the build-up, Ciara. Sometimes it's the journey, not the destination.'

Usually her father made more sense, but Ciara realised that this trip back to Toronto to sort out his recently deceased father's house was not as exciting for him as it was for her. 'This trip is different, Dad,' she said.

He nodded. 'Yeah, I guess it is, at that.'

Just then Ciara's mobile phone pinged to indicate a text message. Instinctively she went to reach for the phone, but her father smiled and pointed at it. 'You know the rule!'

'Don't interrupt a conversation to text,' intoned Ciara, mimicking Dad's deep voice and Canadian accent.

'Got it in one!' he said.

Even though her father worked in software development and was more tech-savvy than most of her friends' parents, he had strong views about mobile phone etiquette. Secretly Ciara felt he had a point when he claimed that manners hadn't always kept up with technology, though of course she didn't admit this to his face. And in fairness he was pretty cool most of the time – her friends had been really impressed when he had performed songs by Neil Young and Gordon Lightfoot on his guitar at the Residents' Day barbeque.

'Anyway,' he said now, 'we'll be in Canada in seven hours.'

'And two hours after that we'll be in Lakefield,' said Ciara, unable to keep the excitement from her voice.

Dad reached out and squeezed her hand affectionately. 'Don't get your hopes up too high, honey. We don't know what we're going to find.'

'It has to be something big, Dad, for it to be kept secret all these years.'

'Maybe,' he conceded.

Before they could discuss it any further, a tannoy sounded and their flight was called.

'OK,' said Dad, rising from his seat in the coffee dock, 'next stop Toronto.'

'Right,' said Ciara. Then she rose and followed him, eager to reach Canada and to get to the bottom of a mystery that was almost ninety years old.

CHAPTER TWO

Lake Katchewanooka, Ontario, Canada

25 June 1928

Mike knew that they would be trespassing, but that made landing on Webster Island an adventure. He kept his hand steady on the tiller, a gentle breeze tossing his hair as the boat glided over the surface of the sparkling water. He loved being out on the lake on hot summer days, and he savoured his sun-kissed surroundings, recalling how the same landscape looked with the lake frozen and the island and shoreline buried under snow. Mike was a boy who enjoyed contrasts, the warmth of the sun on his shoulders today all the sweeter after the numbing cold of winter. His musings on the seasons were cut short when the other occupant of the small sailing skiff spoke up nervously.

'Are you sure we should do this?'

Mike looked towards the bow of the boat where Wilson Taggart sat. Wilson was the same age as Mike, but he was skinny and small for a twelve-year-old, whereas Mike was well built and tall. 'Of course we shouldn't, the island's private property,' he answered with a grin, 'but that's half the fun, isn't it?'

'Is it?'

'Relax, Will, there's no-one living there. And we won't be seen. We'll sail round the island and approach from the far side.'

'OK. It's just…I don't want to get into trouble with the school – or with your dad.'

Mike shook his head. 'He has better things to worry about than us going to an empty island. Anyway, no-one's going to know.'

'I just thought that someone could track us if they were watching from the shoreline with binoculars.'

'Who's likely to do that?'

'Well…I guess it's not that likely.'

'Exactly,' said Mike. 'Look, we could be hit by lightning, we could be, I don't know, swallowed by a whale! I could have a heart attack and you could have a stroke!'

Mike was rewarded by a smile from Wilson, and he grinned back. 'Don't meet your troubles halfway, Will, that's what my ma always says. Most things that people worry about never happen. That's another of her gems!'

Wilson considered this, and nodded. 'That's probably true.'

'Of course, I don't do everything she says,' added Mike quickly, not wanting to sound like a mammy's boy, 'but she's right on that one.'

'I know she's not a teacher, but she seems smarter than half the teachers in the school.'

'Don't say that to her, she'll get a swelled head!' answered Mike. But even as he laughed off the compliment, he couldn't help but feel pleased on his mother's behalf. There was no doubt that Ma was smart, though she would never have the opportunity to qualify as a teacher in The Grove School.

Mike looked back over his shoulder towards The Grove. It was a private college on the outskirts of the town of Lakefield and a three-hour train journey from Toronto. It was regarded as one of the top schools in Ontario, and perhaps in all of Canada. It educated the sons of the wealthy and powerful, and boys came as boarders, both from abroad and from throughout Canada. Mike's father worked there as a janitor, and his mother was a nurse who ran the school infirmary. Mike's parents could not afford the fees at The Grove, and so he attended the local school in Lakefield.

By contrast, Wilson had no money problems. He was a member of the Taggart clan, a family of wealthy steel magnates who had emigrated from Antrim in Northern Ireland in the previous century, and made a fortune in Canada's booming steel industry. Mike's family had also left Ireland, though only five years ago, and Mike still had memories of leaving their home in Dublin as a seven-year-old.

But although the Taggarts were enormously wealthy and influential, Mike had no sense of inferiority. As a matter of fact, he felt sorry for Wilson.

He looked at the other boy now, who was in high-quality casual clothes that made him look slightly overdressed for a summer boat trip. Mike had just got to know him this week, and he reckoned that his own friends in Lakefield would regard Wilson as posh, and even a figure of fun. But although the other boy was rich and well spoken, he wasn't stuck up, and Mike felt that despite being a bit timid he was still interesting.

Normally Mike didn't mix much with students at The Grove, even though his family was provided with a house on the school grounds. Wilson's case was different, however, in that he had stayed on after school had broken up for summer holidays the previous weekend. With all his fellow pupils gone back to their families, Wilson had been left alone because of some complication in his father's business, which had delayed his arrival to collect Wilson.

Mike had been a little put out at first when his mother had taken the solitary boy under her wing, inviting him to their family home, and suggesting that Mike go sailing with him in one of the school boats. But as he got to know Wilson he was impressed by how many quirky facts he knew about popular music, and history, and sport. And when it emerged that they shared an interest in the latest craze of flying, with both of them hero-worshipping Charles Lindbergh, who had flown non-stop from America to Paris, a friendship had begun to emerge.

It would only be temporary, Mike knew, and once Mr Taggart arrived in Lakefield he would whisk Wilson away on holiday to some fancy resort. Meanwhile though, Mike was enjoying getting to know a boy whose background was so different to his own.

Dad had warned him to be polite and not to question Wilson too much, but Mike was naturally curious and there were lots of things he wondered about. Like why did business come first with Mr Taggart, leaving his son stranded at The Grove? Or, with his mother dead, why had Wilson not been invited by any aunts or uncles to stay with them until his father could collect him? Because what was the use in being rich if you ended up on your own when you should be on holidays?

A wave slapped the side of the boat and Mike realised that his mind had been drifting. He swung the tiller, correcting his line of approach. Despite his father's warning not to be too nosy he was fascinated by Wilson's unusual situation. But he would go carefully, he decided, and not rush things or make the other boy uncomfortable. Instead he sat back in the boat now, enjoying the glorious June sunshine as he kept on course for the island.

CHAPTER THREE

Pearson International Airport, Toronto

April 2015

The scream of the jet's engines grew louder as the 757 touched down; Ciara knew that the pilot was applying reverse thrust to slow the plane as it hurtled down the runway.

She had loved aeroplanes from the first time she had gone up in one as a three-year-old, and a career as a pilot was right at the top of her list of jobs, alongside writing best-selling mystery novels. And maybe she could do both. After all, pilots on trans-Atlantic stopovers must have time on their hands in hotel rooms, and that time could surely be used for writing.

Right now, though, her usual excitement at a smooth landing was overshadowed by the excitement of her mission. She loved the word mission, and thought it wasn't an exaggeration to use it to describe her task of getting to the bottom of the mystery surrounding Granddad. Ciara thought he had been the coolest granddad of any of her friends, and she had been really sad when he died the previous year at the amazing age of ninety-eight.

How mad must it have been to be born in 1916, when there was no such thing as television, no mobile phones, no computers? Granddad had even shown her a scrapbook with a signed photograph of Amelia Earhart, the first woman to fly the Atlantic. Ciara wondered if her interest in flying had its roots in her grandfather telling her stories about the pioneering days, when people like Charles Lindbergh and Amelia Earhart were aviation's early superstars.

Her thoughts were suddenly interrupted when her father spoke. 'So, Ciara, marks out of ten?' he asked, smiling.

'Smooth landing, I gave him an eight.'

'I'm sure he'd be thrilled,' said Dad with a grin.

The 757 had slowed down now and was taxiing in, and all around her Ciara could see people switching on their mobile phones. She turned her own on but the only message was from the local telephone network. Just then the steward came on the intercom and welcomed everyone to Canada.

'Nice to be home, Dad?' she said.

'Yeah. Though Dublin is home now, really.'

Ciara knew that as a young man her father had travelled from Canada to Dublin to study. It was where he had met Mam, after which they had got married and settled in the suburb of Seapoint, where Ciara grew up with her brother and sister. Ciara loved Seapoint, and knew its every nook and cranny. Dad must surely have similar feelings about Lakefield, where he had grown up.

'It'll still be good to go back though, won't it?'

'Kinda bittersweet, Ciara. It's my hometown and I've lots of happy memories of it. But Lakefield without Granddad – it'll feel strange.'

Ciara felt a stab of affection for her father and she reached out and squeezed his hand. It had been strange late last year when all the family had flown over for Granddad's funeral, with the empty house seeming weird without his familiar presence. It had taken until now to sort our all the legal details of Granddad's estate, and Ciara was coming back with her father to keep him company as he signed off on the legal paperwork and put the house up for sale. But there was another reason for her making the trip.

She had shared with her grandfather a love of puzzles, and in his will he had left a letter addressed to Ciara. It was only to be given to her by his lawyer when all other legalities were finalised. Some of her family had assumed that it was a piece of advice, or a poem, or a farewell note to his youngest grandchild, but Ciara suspected otherwise.

Granddad had been renowned for his love of mysteries. He read lots of crime novels and often claimed to solve the puzzle before the end of the book. The last summer that she had visited him, Granddad had mentioned that his boyhood contained an incident that had been kept secret ever since. In his mid-nineties he was the last of his circle still living, but when Ciara had pressed him for details he had said that he couldn't break a sworn agreement not to disclose what had happened. But then he had smiled mischievously and said that if someone good at solving mysteries were to unravel the clues to the story after he was dead, that would be a different matter. Ciara had been wondering ever since. What on earth could he have kept hidden for nearly ninety years?

The plane came to a standstill, and passengers immediately began unbuckling their belts. Ciara quickly undid hers, and her father looked at her and smiled.

'Eager to get going?'

'Can't wait, Dad,' she answered. 'Can't wait!'

CHAPTER FOUR

Lake Katchewanooka, Ontario, Canada

June 25th 1928

Wilson felt excited as the boat drew near to the heavily wooded island. Normally he would be nervous of trespassing, but Mike's carefree attitude had affected him, and now he felt pleased by his own daring. Mike had made the island trip feel like fun, calling out *Land Ho!* and other mock-pirate phrases, and Wilson had entered into the spirit of the thing, replying in his best attempt at a pirate accent.

This must be what it was like to have an older brother, he thought, and he wished that he wasn't an only child. Of course, Mike wasn't actually any older than him, just bigger and stronger. And it wasn't anyone's fault that he was an only child – his mother had died giving birth to a sister who didn't survive, so it was just Wilson and his father now. But being allied with Mike, even temporarily, made him feel somehow protected, and so he felt bolder.

It was a good feeling, and he envied other boys in the school who had brothers to give them moral support and prevent them being bullied. Most of the boys in his class had been sympathetic when they heard he wasn't spending the holidays at home. A couple of them, though, had made smart remarks, and Moose Packham, a nasty boy from the class above Wilson, had said that his father mustn't want him if he was abandoning him during the school holidays.

Wilson had denied this vehemently, but he had still been hurt by the comment. And a small part of him was disappointed that his father's business commitments always came first, even though he understood that, as Managing Director of Taggart Industries, Dad had a demanding job.

He wished that his father had invited him to come to Ohio, where he was negotiating with a group of steel mills that Taggart Industries wanted to buy. But Dad didn't think it professional to have his son along on an important business trip. Normally Wilson could have gone to stay with his father's sister, Victoria, at Cobourg. This summer, however, Aunt Vickie was keeping up the Taggart tradition of maintaining contact with Northern Ireland, and had gone with her husband and servants to spend a month at the old family estate in County Antrim.

'OK, Will, mooring rope ready?' cried Mike, cutting short Wilson's musings.

'Mooring rope ready, Captain!'

Mike was lowering the sail and pointing. 'See that grassy bank up ahead?'

'Yes.'

'Jump ashore when I bring us alongside, and moor us to a tree.'

'All right!' answered Wilson more confidently than he felt. Although he could swim well, he wasn't athletic, and he hoped he could jump from the moving boat and land safely on the bank.

Mike gave him a thumbs up, and the gesture lifted his spirits.

He was really glad that Nurse Farrelly had taken him under her wing and introduced him to Mike, her son. He would have preferred not to be stranded in Lakefield, but spending time with Mike proved a consolation.

Wilson was realistic enough to know that, as wealthy Protestants, the Taggarts wouldn't normally mix with working-class Catholics like the Farrellys. Even though both families had originally come from Ireland, his father would see their differing religions as a big bar. That – and the gap in social class – meant that Dad would see more differences between them than common ground.

But although he rarely contradicted his father, Wilson felt he was too rigid on things like that. Why write someone off just because they were a different religion, or they weren't as rich as you were?

'All right, Will, stand by to board!'

'Standing by, Captain!'

Mike skilfully drew the boat close to the grassy bank, and Wilson rose and crouched in the bow. He balanced himself and gauged the gap between the moving craft and the shore. He was anxious not to capsize the boat.

'Ready?!'

'Yes!'

'Go!'

Wilson hesitated, the gap still seeming wide to him. Then he grasped the mooring rope tighter and leaped for the bank. Please God, he thought as he jumped, let me not look like a fool! His prayer was answered in part, in that he made the grassy bank, but he landed awkwardly. As he was falling, he saw a small tree stump. At full stretch he managed to throw the mooring rope over it, and pull it tight, before rolling to a stop himself.

'Well done, Will!' cried Mike as he used the mooring line to pull the boat alongside the bank.

'Thanks,' answered Wilson. He grinned, pleased. He sensed that his adventures with Mike were just beginning.

Lucy froze, her charcoal pencil halfway to her sketching pad. She was sitting on a tree stump in a sun-dappled glade on Webster Island, her canoe hidden nearby under heavy foliage. But now the snap of a twig had alerted her to the presence of – what? An animal, another person? She listened intently. The sound had been some distance away, but it had been a clear snap, which suggested something heavier than a rabbit or a fox.

She would need to be careful if there was a bear nearby, especially if it was a mother with cubs. But there could be problems, too, if it was a person. Lucy knew that some people disliked the Ojibwe and other Indian tribes. She thought that this was silly, although she knew that some members of her tribe could also be narrow-minded about outsiders. But leaving the Ojibwe Reserve and coming onto Webster Island without permission could mean trouble.

Only if I'm caught, she thought, rising quickly but silently. She swiftly put away her charcoal pencil and gathered her possessions. Just then she heard voices in the distance, and she realised that they were coming in her direction. Her instinct was to make for the canoe but she forced herself not to panic. The canoe was hidden back in the direction from which the voices had come, and if she made for it now she might run headlong into the people she wanted to avoid.

She heard a laugh, then more chatter. The people were still coming her way. But the voices sounded like boys rather than adults. Even so it would be better not to encounter them. She looked around for a hiding place. There was thicker foliage inland from the glade, and Lucy clutched her easel to her chest and began to make for it. Just then she heard a whoop, and it became clear that the boys were racing along the trail towards the glade. She could hear the sound of their steps, and she realised that she wasn't going to make it into hiding before they reached her. She hesitated briefly then made her decision. Better to face them confidently than to be caught scurrying away. She turned about, walked briskly back to the tree stump and put her gear on the ground.

A few seconds later two boys of about her own age burst laughingly into the clearing. One was well built and had floppy brown hair, the other was smaller with dark, neatly quiffed hair. Both boys started in shock on seeing Lucy.

'God! What are you doing here?' asked the taller boy.

'What are *you* doing here?' she countered.

'We're, eh…we're exploring.'

'We took a sailboat out for a picnic,' added the smaller boy.

'Are you from the reserve?' asked the first one.

With her olive skin, jet-black braided hair and buckskin clothes, Lucy knew it was obvious that she was Ojibwe. She nodded.

'If they caught you here, you'd be up for trespassing.'

Lucy felt a stab of irritation. '*Trespassing*? All this land was *ours* – before the government took it!'

The taller boy looked at her a moment, then nodded. 'I hadn't thought about it like that. Fair point.'

Lucy had been expecting him to argue and she found herself disarmed by his surprising response.

'But since the treaties, the reserve land is yours, right?' said the smaller boy. 'And now this belongs to someone else.'

Lucy was about to rail against the injustice of the treaties, but the boy held up his hands as though in surrender. 'I'm not saying that's fair. But that's what they'd claim.'

'And I wasn't trying to be smart about trespassing,' said the first boy. 'I'm just saying you could get into trouble.'

'So could *you*, then,' answered Lucy. 'You're trespassing too, aren't you?'

The taller boy smiled. 'Yeah. But if you don't tell on us, we won't tell on you!'

He had laughing blue eyes and his smile was infectious. Lucy found herself smiling back.

'OK, then,' she said.

'So what brought you out here?' asked the smaller boy.

'Sketching,' said Lucy indicating her drawing gear on the ground

'What do you sketch?' queried the other boy.

'Anything I fancy.'

'Can you just draw anything you see?'

'Yeah, pretty much.'

'Gosh, I can't draw for nuts! I'd love to be able to do that.'

'Could you draw us?' asked the smaller boy. He was more serious-looking than his companion, but his eyes were bright with curiosity, and Lucy sensed a lively mind at work.

'Of course.'

'How long would that take?'

Lucy shrugged. 'Not long. But I don't think–'

'Go on then! Do us!' said the bigger boy.

Lucy hesitated, and the second boy looked her playfully in the eye. 'You said you could draw anything.'

Even though his tone was friendly, there was an element of challenge in it, and Lucy found it hard to resist a challenge. She knew she was a good artist, and sometimes to amuse her mother she drew caricatures of people on the reserve. OK, she thought, let's see how they'd like that.

'You're sure you want to see what I make of you?' she asked.

'Yes!' they both replied.

'All right,' said Lucy, then she set up her easel, told the smaller boy to be still and began to sketch him with sure, quick strokes.

CHAPTER FIVE

Ciara felt her heartbeat getting faster as she neared Lakefield.

The rental car that Dad had picked up at Toronto airport had sped along a sunlit Highway 401, then taken them north, towards the Kawartha Lakes country, bringing them past Millbrook and Peterborough. Now they were on the outskirts of Lakefield, and Dad was turning smoothly into the drive of his old home.

Coming to stay in Granddad's house had always been exciting, but Ciara knew that this time would feel different. It would be strange to stay in the house without the cheery presence of her grandfather. Yet this visit would be fascinating, as she got to grips with the puzzle he had left.

Dad pulled to a halt now as they reached the top of the driveway. It was a family tradition that they always played Gordon Lightfoot songs on the journey to Lakefield – though Dad had agreed to a batch of current songs from Ciara's tablet while they were driving the 401 – and now he reached forward and faded down the music from *Summer Side of Life,* his all-time favourite album.

Even after years of car journeys together, Ciara had to smile when her father faded a song instead of turning the music off. He claimed that switching an artist off midstream was too abrupt. Ciara knew that some people would think this was mad, but she regarded it as one of the endearingly quirky things that made Dad who he was.

Having faded the song, he turned off the engine and turned to face Ciara. 'Well, here we are.'

'Yeah,' she answered, taking in her surroundings in the soft evening sunshine.

The house and garden looked the same as ever – well tended, yet lived in. But nobody had been living here since Granddad died, and Ciara realised that some arrangement must have been made with the neighbours to maintain the property. She looked at the porch on which her grandfather used to sit in his rocking chair and suddenly she was hit by a sense of loss. She had thought that she had done all her crying at the time of the funeral, but now she felt a lump in her throat as she stared at the empty porch.

As though reading her mind, Dad reached out and took her hand. 'I miss him too, honey,' he said softly.

'He was great, wasn't he?'

'Sure was. They broke the mould when they made Mike Farrelly.'

Ciara was struck by a troubling thought and she slowly turned to her father. 'I hope...' Ciara bit her lip and looked at Dad, unsure how to proceed.

'What?'

'I hope I don't find out anything that would...'

'That would what?' prompted Dad gently.

'I've been dying to read Granddad's letter and solve this mystery. But just supposing the reason he kept it secret was...well, because it was something bad? I want to be able to remember Granddad the way he was.'

Her father looked thoughtful for a moment before replying.

'I haven't a clue what's in the letter, Ciara, or what happened all those years ago. All I know – and I know this for sure – is that he was a great father, and a good man.'

'So whatever the secret is, you think it will be OK?'

'Yes, I do.' He squeezed her hand softly 'All right?'

'Yeah. Yeah, I think that too, Dad.'

'Good. And Ciara?'

'Yes?'

'Anytime you need to talk…about anything…I'm always here.'

'I know. Thanks, Dad.'

' So…will we head inside?'

Ciara nodded, then, without any further hesitation, she unstrapped her belt and stepped out of the car.

CHAPTER SIX

'**L**et's see how you do it!' said Mike, moving to join the girl as she sketched Wilson with quick strokes.

'No,' she said. She held up her hand to stop him coming around her side of the easel. 'You have to be patient. I'll show you when it's finished.'

Mike was about to respond, but she looked him in the eye.

'This is the way I work,' she said.

Her tone was matter of fact but firm, and Mike sensed that there was no use arguing.

'Are you always this bossy?' he asked.

'Are you always this pushy?' she replied.

Mike grinned despite himself, liking her feisty attitude. 'OK then,' he conceded, 'you're the artist!'

'That's right,' she answered, but she said it good humouredly, and Mike sensed that she might be fun.

'Can I scratch my face?' asked Wilson.

'I know I said be still, but you don't have to be a statue.'

The air was scented with wild flowers, and Mike relaxed and watched as Wilson scratched his cheek, then adopted a formal pose again. He *did* look a bit like a statue, Mike thought, then he realised that the girl had finished.

'What's your name?' she asked. 'I'll put it on the sketch.'

'Wilson.'

'No, your first name.'

'Wilson *is* my first name.'

'Oh, sounds likes a surname.'

'It's a surname as well. It was my mother's name.'

'Your mother's first name was Wilson too?'

Wilson laughed. 'No! Her first name was Emily. She was Emily Wilson and she married my father, Trevor Taggart. So I'm Wilson Taggart.'

'Right.'

'My people come from Northern Ireland,' explained Wilson, 'and there's a tradition. Boys are given their mother's surname as a first name.'

'Why do they do that?' asked the girl, and despite his eagerness to see the finished drawing Mike found himself curious to hear the answer too.

Wilson looked thoughtful. 'Well…I've never actually asked. But I suppose it's a way of respecting the mother's family name. Even though she changes her name when she marries, her surname gets to live on.'

'I like that tradition,' said the girl. 'And what about you?' she said turning to Mike.

'Our family is simpler. My da is Thomas Farrelly, my ma is Hannah Farrelly and I'm Mike Farrelly.'

'What was your mother called before she married?'

'Hannah McGinty. And I'm really glad I wasn't called McGinty!' he added.

'I'm sorry, we should have introduced ourselves,' said Wilson, and Mike was amused by the other boy's formality.

'What's your name?' he asked now, turning to the girl.

'Lucy. Lucy Neadeau.'

'Neadeau?' said Wilson. 'Sounds French.'

'It might sound French, but I'm pure Ojibwe,' she answered proudly.

'Good for you,' said Mike. 'So, Lucy Neadeau, can we see the picture now?'

'Yes, let me just add the name.' She quickly wrote with the charcoal pencil, then took the drawing off the easel and turned it around.

Mike looked at the sketch and burst out laughing.

'God, do I really look like that?' asked Wilson in mock horror.

'It's a caricature, an exaggeration,' said Lucy.

Mike could see that she had focussed on Wilson's stiffness and exaggerated it even more, but although it was humorous, she had also somehow caught his essence. 'You're brilliant at this,' he said. 'How do you do it?'

'You pick a couple of things and… sort of blow them up. I don't think about it too much, I just go with it.'

Lucy handed the drawing to Wilson. 'No hard feelings?'

'No hard feelings. In fact, it *is* kind of funny.'

'Glad you've a sense of humour,' said Lucy, then she turned to

Mike. 'Now it's your turn.'

Mike grimaced playfully. 'Not sure what I'm letting myself in for.'

'Just be still for a minute,' she answered, then she slipped a fresh sheet of paper onto the easel and began to work in quick strokes.

'You're really fast,' said Wilson admiringly.

Lucy nodded without stopping the work. 'Fast is good with caricatures.'

Mike stayed unmoving and tried not to be as stiff as Wilson had been, but still he was relieved when Lucy finally said 'OK, you can relax.'

He was curious to see how Lucy had turned his features into a caricature and he saw that she had a slightly mischievous grin on her face.

'Ready?' she asked.

'As I'll ever be.'

She turned the drawing around, and this time it was Wilson who laughed aloud.

Mike saw that Lucy had exaggerated his freckles and floppy hair, but although again the drawing was humorous, she had managed to capture his appearance.

He put up his hands as though surrendering. 'You got me!'

Lucy smiled and handed him the drawing. 'I like a subject who's a good sport.'

'A *subject*?' said Mike. 'You have all the artist lingo, haven't you?'

'Of course,' answered Lucy. ' If you're going to be an artist you have to talk like one.'

'You're really talented, Lucy,' said Wilson.

'Thank you.'

'Will you go to art college when you leave school?'

Mike felt slightly embarrassed, and thought that Wilson's question was a little insensitive. Was he really so wealthy and privileged that he had no idea of how life was in the real world? Mike knew that many Indians spent their whole lives on reserves, hunting and fishing and trying to get by as best they could. The idea that Lucy would go to college to study art showed how little Wilson was aware of life outside his circle.

'I hope to go to college,' answered Lucy. 'One of my teachers is backing me.'

'Yeah?' said Mike, trying to hide his surprise.

'She says I have real talent. But I need a good portfolio if I'm to win a scholarship.'

'What's a portfolio?'

'A collection of an artist's work,' answered Wilson.

'Anyway, that's what I'm doing this summer,' explained Lucy. 'I go out collecting herbs, but I bring my art gear with me, so I do a drawing or a painting every day. Over the summer I plan to explore this whole area, and go somewhere different each day.'

'Sounds great,' said Mike.

'Yeah, it does,' agreed Wilson. 'Maybe… No, forget it.'

'What?' asked Lucy.

'Maybe we could do it together? Go somewhere new each morning as an adventure?'

Lucy didn't answer at once, and Mike could see that Wilson was embarrassed.

'Of course, that mightn't…that mightn't suit you,' he said, blabbering slightly. 'I didn't mean to impose, I just–'

'I wouldn't mind,' said Lucy. 'Could be fun. But your families mightn't want you hanging around with an Indian.'

'Nothing wrong with being friends with Indians,' said Mike.

'Of course not. I'm proud to be Ojibwe, but some people still look down on us.'

'Not me,' said Mike.

'Or me,' added Wilson.

But if he was honest, Mike reckoned that his father might actually have a problem. Da was a fair, decent man, but he was conservative, and he might say that it was better to leave the Ojibwe to their own ways. Still, maybe there was a way around that…

'I've just had a brainwave,' he said. 'Supposing we don't tell any adults. It could be like a secret club. Then it wouldn't matter what anyone thought!' He looked at Lucy mischievously. 'What do you say?'

She grinned. 'Yeah. Yeah, I like it.'

'What would we call ourselves?' asked Wilson.

'Lucy, Mike and Wilson!' said Lucy.

Wilson laughed with the others, but returned to his idea. 'Seriously though, if we have a secret club it should have a name.'

'*Giimoodad. The Giimoodad Club*,' said Lucy.

'What's a giimoodad?' asked Wilson.

'It's the Ojibwe word for a secret.'

'Brilliant!' said Mike.

Lucy looked to Wilson.

'Yes, I really like it.'

'All right, the Giimoodad Club it is!' said Mike. 'The G Club for short. Let's shake on it.'

Mike offered his right hand to Lucy and his left hand to Wilson, and Lucy and Wilson reached over to close the circle and take each other's free hands. It felt silly but fun and they burst into laughter as they shook hands.

As the three stood happily in the sunlit glade, Mike had a sudden premonition that this was an important moment. He didn't know how long their club might last, or where it would take them, but something told him he wouldn't forget this day – the day they formed the G Club.

CHAPTER SEVEN

Ciara sat alone in her grandfather's study. Dad had driven into town to get flapjacks and maple syrup – another tradition whenever he returned to Canada – but she was tired after the long flight, and was happy to stay in the house.

It was six in the evening, Canadian time, and although she was slightly tired, in truth she wanted to have time here on her own. The mystery regarding Granddad felt within reach now that she was in Lakefield, and of all the rooms in her grandfather's rambling house, this study was the one that seemed to reflect his life the most.

And what a life it had been. He had been born during the First World War, had fought in the Second World War, been around for the arrival of penicillin, nuclear power, rock and roll. He had been a boy when ancient tunes like 'Ol' Man River' and 'Me and My Shadow' were the latest hits, he had seen the early aviators who flew planes with wooden wings, and the astronauts who flew rockets to the moon.

She looked around the study, its walls filled with framed photographs and drawings that captured the many phases of her grandfather's life. She had always simply thought of him as Granddad, but now, if she were to unravel a puzzle, she needed to study him more carefully.

So which was the essential Mike Farrelly? she wondered as she rose from her chair and looked closely at the photographs. Was it the tousle-haired boy, grinning into the camera with his family in black and white photographs, or the dashing World War Two fighter pilot? The bachelor who married late but then became a dedicated family man? The college lecturer, the gardener, the loving grandfather?

She saw pictures of Granddad with other staff members in Trent University, on his wedding day with his pretty young wife, pictures of Dad as an only child with his obviously doting parents, pictures of an older Granddad and Granny with Ciara's brother and sister, Connor and Sarah. Granny had died the year Ciara was born, so there were no photographs of them together, but there was a really nice picture of a seven-year-old Ciara with Granddad, mounted beside a framed poster of Charles Lindbergh, which was signed by the aviator himself.

There were faded charcoal drawings of Webster Island, of Lakefield's main street, and of Young's Point, and an old sepia print of Ciara's great-grandfather, Thomas Farrelly, who looked stiffly into the camera, dressed in the uniform of a corporal in the Dublin Fusiliers.

There was a whole life laid out on these walls, but so far no hint as to what Granddad's secret might be. According to her father, Granddad didn't keep a personal diary, so she couldn't count on getting that kind of insight when they met the solicitor tomorrow morning for the final hand-over of all paperwork.

Ciara moved back along the wall to the black-and-white photos of the Farrelly family in the 1920s. In some of the photos of Granddad with Patrick and Edith, his long-dead brother and sister, he looked about the same age as Ciara was now, and in all the pictures, he was grinning, his floppy hair and freckled face giving him a roguish look. What did you do, Granddad, what was your big secret? thought Ciara.

She heard the sound of Dad's car coming up the drive and her reverie was broken. She moved towards the study door, knowing she ought to set the table for supper. Her mind was racing, however, and she wished it was tomorrow, when she would be one step nearer to unravelling the past.

CHAPTER EIGHT

'Come on, Da,' said Mike, 'be a sport – please!'

'It's not a question of being a sport, it's about striking a balance.'

They were in the Farrellys' kitchen, the late afternoon sunlight streaming in the window and back-lighting his father's bulky frame as he sat sipping a mug of strong black coffee.

Mike's mother was peeling potatoes for the evening meal, to which Mike wanted to invite his new friend Wilson. Mike had enjoyed the time with Wilson today more than he expected, and meeting Lucy and forming the G Club had been great fun – with the additional thrill of the club being a secret.

'He's not a bit stuck up, Da,' he added now. 'He wouldn't be looking down his nose at us.'

'So well he might!' said Mike's mother, but she said it with a smile, and Mike sensed that Ma wouldn't mind the other boy joining them. With his older brother and sister living and work-ing in Peterborough, Mike reckoned there was ample room for one more at the dinner table.

'I'm not saying Wilson is stuck up,' said Da. 'But the Taggarts are a different kind of family.'

'They're richer, that's all.'

'It's not all, Mike. They're Protestants, they're powerful, they're landowners back in Ireland.'

'What people were back in Ireland shouldn't affect us here in Canada, Da.'

'That's not the way the world is. They're one type, we're another – moving to Canada doesn't change that.'

But it *should* change that, Mike thought. Canada was supposed to be a country where people could make a fresh start. It was the reason his own parents had come here. Although a qualified carpenter, Da had found it hard to get steady work in Dublin, and for a time they had had to live on Ma's earnings as a nurse in Stewart's Hospital.

Mike remembered how it had felt like an adventure coming to Canada, where everything seemed bigger and more spacious. It hadn't all gone smoothly at first, and for a while he had been ridiculed for his Irish accent. Even though his outgoing personality had soon won him new friends in Lakefield – and he had quickly acquired his present Canadian accent – he remembered how it was to feel like an outsider. It was why he didn't want to see Wilson on his own now.

'Anyway, what's brought on this change of mind?' asked Da. 'You weren't so keen on sailing with him before.'

'I've gotten to know him better. He's really interesting.'

'Look, Ma's heart was in the right place, as usual, but–'

'Thank you, kind sir,' said Ma. 'Write that down, Mike, God knows when I'll get praised again!'

Mike smiled at his mother's antics, but his father put down his mug of coffee and spoke seriously. 'What I'm saying is that it's good to help a boy whose father can't be…well…let's say, *around* for his son. So we look out for Wilson, but without overstepping the mark. He's not one of us.'

'I know what you're saying, Da. But he's back in his room, all on his own.'

Mike could see that his good-natured father was torn, then Ma spoke up. 'One dinner in a family environment, Tom — it's not going to change the world. And if it was Mike, we'd like someone to be nice to him.'

Da shook his head and smiled wryly. 'The pair of you will badger me till I give in, won't you?'

'Yeah, pretty much!' said Mike, delighted that Da was giving way.

'Did anyone ever tell you you're a pest?' asked his father.

'Did anyone ever tell me I'm the best?' said Mike, pretending to mishear.

'Go on, you scamp,' said Da, rising from the table and mussing Mike's hair.

'Thanks, Da, I'll tell him now!'

'One dinner, mind. We're not doing it every day.'

'As you say yourself, Da, we'll play that by ear!'

His father was about to respond, but Mike had already laughed and run happily through the door.

* * *

Wilson shielded the light from his flashlight so it wouldn't be seen, as he sat up in bed in the darkened dormitory. It was unlikely that the duty teacher would catch him – with all the other pupils gone home on holidays the dormitory was empty – but he didn't want to take the chance.

It was eleven o'clock at night now, and the school was quiet, with just the faint sound of the breeze audible in the trees as it blew in from Lake Katchewanooka. Wilson was tired after his day out on the lake with Mike, but his mind was racing and after such an eventful day he wasn't quite ready to sleep. Forming the secret G Club had been exciting, and he had really enjoyed the family dinner that he had shared with the Farrellys.

Wilson knew Mr Farrelly to see from his job as school janitor. As janitor he tended to look a little strict, but tonight he had been at ease when eating with his family. Mrs Farrelly was good fun – like Mike – and Wilson had been struck by the difference in his own family situation.

As soon as he thought it he had felt guilty. It wasn't Dad's fault that Mum had died, leaving the two of them on their own. Dad was decent and fair in most of his dealings, and Wilson recognised that he had his best interests at heart. It was just that eating with the Farrellys had opened his eyes to a type of family life different to his own, but really attractive. Maybe they would ask him again to dinner now that he had made friends with Mike. He certainly hoped so, though it would be bad manners to push the matter.

He shifted the flashlight onto the ledger he was writing up. He didn't write up entries every night, only when interesting things happened to him – like today's adventures with Lucy and Mike – or when important events occurred in the outside world.

In recent times there were entries about Lindbergh crossing the Atlantic, the arrival of talking movies, and oil being discovered in the Middle East. Just last week there had been an announcement of the death of the famous Mrs Pankhurst, who had led the campaign in Britain for votes for women.

Wilson loved recording the sense of progress happening and the world changing – mostly for the better, it seemed to him. Some day his ledgers would be a record of all that. Maybe he would even write a book when he was older.

Now, though, he was finished. He carefully placed the ledger on the wooden section beside his bench. He locked the chest and placed the key in his pocket, from habit. He wasn't going to lose another ledger, the way he had when Moose Packham had thrown one of them into the lake.

Packham was two years older than Wilson, and much bigger, and Wilson had felt furious and humiliated by the bully's nasty action. Standing up to Moose wasn't an option, however, and would only have added a beating to the humiliation.

Moose was a strong football and hockey player, and as such was admired but also feared by many of the boys in The Grove School. His standing had risen earlier in the year when he had saved a dog from drowning in the freezing waters of the lake. But if he was kind to animals, he could be cruel to other boys, and he didn't like Wilson.

Wilson's crime – apart from being a 'measly bookworm,' as Moose described him – was to come from a long-established, wealthy family. By contrast, Moose's father, Brent Packham, had made his fortune more recently, running a brewery and transport company in Peterborough and, it was whispered, smuggling alcohol across the Canadian border into the USA, where its sale was still prohibited.

All of the pupils in The Grove came from well-off backgrounds, but there was still an unspoken pecking order, and Wilson guessed that Moose Peckham resented being thought of as vulgar 'new money.'

It was Moose who had hit a nerve in claiming that Wilson's father mustn't care about his son if he was leaving him in the school. Of course, as things turned out, he wouldn't have met Mike and Lucy if he hadn't been staying on in the school this week. Still, Dad hadn't known that Wilson would make two new friends, and he couldn't shake off the feeling that maybe there was a grain of truth in Moose Packham's comments. No, he told himself, that wasn't fair. Dad loved him.

Determined not to feel sad, he thought instead about the caricatures that Lucy Neadeau had done. She was brilliant at drawing, but she was also clever in the way she had exaggerated his serious features. There was something really funny, too, in how she had made Mike look like a freckle-faced, wide-eyed scarecrow.

He smiled at the memory. He was looking forward to seeing them both in the morning. Then Wilson slipped beneath the blankets on his bed, turned off the flashlight, and lay down to sleep in the empty dormitory.

Part Two

Complications

CHAPTER NINE

Lucy looked at her mother across the kitchen table and suddenly felt bad about deceiving her. But the G Club was just between herself, Mike and Wilson. Mom mightn't approve. Lots of people were prejudiced against the Ojibwe and other tribes, but native people could be prejudiced too, and there were people on her reserve who wouldn't approve of her befriending outsiders.

The Otonabee Reserve was on the shores of Lake Katchawanooka, north of the town of Lakefield. But although the town was only a few miles away, it was a different world, and one that most people on the reserve visited infrequently. In fact any member of the tribe who wanted to leave the reserve was supposed to get permission from the Indian Agent, the government representative who lived in a house near the entrance to it.

Lucy broke this rule when she explored the surrounding lakes and woods. Mom allowed her this mild rebellion against a stupid rule. But she would be worried if she knew that Lucy was socialising with two white boys. It wasn't that Mom herself was narrow-minded, but other people were, and Lucy knew that her mother would think a friendship with outsiders was more trouble than it was worth.

'Hand me the bear oil, would you?' said Mom now.

The morning sunlight streamed in through the windows of their cosy wooden home. The bear oil would be mixed with spruce gum and charcoal and the mixture used to seal the birch bark canoes that were made on the reserve. Canoe-making involved the whole community, with the men carving the wooden laths for the boat, and shaping the birch bark that would be stretched over the frame, and the women sewing the bark tightly to the frame and sealing it with the kind of mixture that Lucy's mother was making.

'Want to help with the canoes, or are you going sketching?' asked Mom.

Lucy hesitated. Canoe-building was one of her favourite jobs – much better than basket-weaving or gutting and selling fish – but she was eager to keep her appointment with her two new friends.

'Is it OK if I sketch this morning and help this afternoon?' she said.

'When most of the work is done?' said her mother with a smile. 'Go on then, but remember who did all the hard work when you're a famous artist!'

'Thanks, Mom,' said Lucy, rising from the table and carrying her breakfast dishes to the sink. She quickly rinsed them before grabbing the coonskin bag containing her sketching gear. 'See you later!' She kissed her mother on the cheek and headed for the door.

She stepped out into the warmth of the summer morning and breathed in the fragrance from the pine trees. The reserve stretched northwards along the lake shore, and looking through the trees, Lucy could see Lake Katchawanooka sparkling in the sunlight. Otonabee wasn't large – it was smaller than Curve Lake Reserve, ten miles distant on the shore of Lake Chemong, where her mother had grown up – but Lucy still thought it was a beautiful place to live.

Nobody in her tribe was rich, with most of the men working as hunters, guides, or labourers in the lumber industry, while the women made black ash baskets and bark mats, and sold fish. But if no-one on the reserve was rich, no-one was starving either; the lack of refrigeration meant that, when animals were killed and skinned, the meat was shared among the families.

Lucy made her way along the trail from her house toward the gathering point in the centre of the reserve. She planned to cut down to the shoreline where her canoe was pulled up on a small beach, but just as she was about to turn she heard a call.

'Hey girl! Not so fast.'

Lucy recognised the voice of Mr Staunton, the Indian Agent. Even though Otonabee Reserve was Ojibwe land, Mr Staunton, as the representative of the government, always used English in his dealings with the inhabitants. He spoke loudly, and had a clipped tone that seemed to go with his stony features and aggressively bushy grey moustache.

Lucy knew not to cross him, and so she turned around at once. Although she normally spoke Ojibwe at home, she was fluent in English, having gone to the reserve school where all education was done through English. It was official policy to replace Ojibwe with English, and Lucy was lucky not to have been sent away from her family, as many children were, to residential schools where anyone caught speaking in the native languages was punished.

'Yes, Mr Staunton?' she said now in a neutral tone, not wanting to sound cheeky, but not wanting to sound too cowed either.

'Where are you headed?'

Mind your own business, was the answer that Lucy longed to give, but she bit her tongue, knowing better than to challenge the Indian Agent openly.

'Just going to do a little fishing. Might catch some bass or walleye,' she explained, not wanting Staunton to know about her sketching, nor about meeting her new friends.

He considered this for a moment then nodded. 'All right.'

Lucy inwardly breathed a sigh of relief. It was an advantage at times to be totally fluent in English, although she still had mixed feelings about it. She was glad of her Ojibwe heritage, yet deep down she knew that English was the language of the future, and was definitely what she would be using if she wanted to be a successful artist.

'Wouldn't mind a bass for supper,' said Staunton. 'Report to my office if you catch one,' he ordered. 'I'll give you twenty cents.'

'Yes, sir.'

'And gut it and wash it before you bring it up.'

I'm not your servant! thought Lucy, but she forced herself to nod in agreement.

'Right, be on your way then.'

Don't hold your breath waiting for that bass, thought Lucy, then she turned away and headed for her canoe, eager to leave behind the Indian Agent, and to meet her new friends.

Mike didn't want to jump off the bridge, but he felt that he had to. Below him the waters of the Otonabee River reflected the clear blue of the summer sky, and a light breeze blew, gently ruffling the surface of the water and making the sunlight glint. The bridge spanned the river at Young's Point, and the drop down to the water was increased by the fact that Mike and Wilson had climbed up onto the metal latticework of the structure.

Earlier the two boys had taken a boat and sailed up Lake Katch-ewanooka to meet Lucy, who had paddled her canoe to join them at Young's Point. It was only the second time that all three of them had met up, but they had quickly resumed the camaraderie of the previous day on Webster Island. They had hailed each other with *Aaniin*, the Ojibwe word for hello, which they had adopted as their club greeting. Sitting companionably on the riverbank, Lucy had done some sketching, Mike had told jokes, and Wilson had excitedly shown them a clipping from his scrapbook about the recent opening of London's Piccadilly tube station. It was a stunning piece of engineering that featured no fewer than *eleven* escalators, and Mike and Lucy shared Wilson's enthusiasm for such a futuristic project.

They had all brought food, to have a picnic later on, but while sketching, Lucy had mentioned that boys from her reserve used the bridge to jump into the river below. Mike was sure that she wasn't trying to score points, and that it was simple curiosity that prompted her to ask if he had ever jumped from the bridge. Even so, it felt a bit lame when he answered no, and before he knew what he was doing he suggested that he and Wilson should try it.

As soon as he said it he could tell that Wilson didn't want to. He felt slightly guilty for railroading his friend into something that scared him. But then again Wilson had been nervous of trespassing on the island yesterday, yet he had been delighted afterwards that they had gone there and formed the G Club.

Before either boy could say anything further, Lucy had said that she would sketch them as they perched on the bridge, in readiness to jump. Seeing her glancing up eagerly, Mike knew there was no going back. He stood looking down at the swirling waters and tried to appear calm as Lucy drew upon her pad with fast confident strokes.

Watching the waters though the latticework of the bridge brought back a memory of his early childhood. Mike remembered holding his father's hand as they looked down at the chilly waters of the River Liffey, just outside his native city of Dublin. It was a similar metal bridge that spanned the Liffey near Palmerston, where Da worked at the time, and Mike recalled feeling deliciously safe as his father had lifted him up to look down at the fast-moving waters of a river swollen by spring rain.

'Gosh, Mike, it feels like a long way down!' said Wilson now, breaking his reverie.

'Just keep your legs together and jump down straight and you'll be all right,' Mike answered. He said it with a confidence he didn't actually feel, and inwardly he cursed himself for impulsively agreeing to jump from the bridge.

Why did he feel that he had to impress Lucy? But even as he asked himself he knew the answer. She was different to any other girl he had met. None of the sisters of his friends carried a Bowie knife in her belt, and none of them could do brilliant drawings like Lucy did.

'OK, I've captured the moment!' she cried now. She lowered her sketch pad and indicated the river. 'Off you go!'

'I don't know about this, Mike,' whispered Wilson.

Mike looked down at the water, and sure enough it did seem like a big jump. He hesitated. If he stayed looking down at the river he was afraid he might lose his nerve, and so he turned to Wilson instead. 'Grab my hand and we'll jump together!'

'I'm not sure...'

'Take my hand. Just do it!' whispered Mike.

Wilson swallowed hard then held out his hand.

Mike grasped his friend's hand, then looked down again.

'Go, boys!' cried Lucy encouragingly.

He looked at her and forced himself to smile. Then he tightened his grip on Wilson's hand.

'OK, Will, let's do it!' he shouted. 'One, two, three!'

And together they jumped, yelling, into the waters of the Otonabee River.

The mouth-watering aroma of frying fish hung in the air,
mixing with the earthy scent from the nearby woods. Wilson sat
back against a tree, his eyes closed as he basked contentedly in the
sunshine. They had chosen a picnic spot along the shoreline of
Clear Lake and fished successfully for walleye. Lucy had gutted the
fish with her Bowie knife, then Mike had fried them in a small
pan.

'OK, grub's up!' he said now, tipping the cooked fish from the
pan onto their plates.

Wilson opened his eyes and sat up, then took a tin plate that
Mike handed to him. This was the life, he thought, out with
friends on a beautiful summer's day. Before him lay Clear Lake, its
calm blue waters stretching way to the horizon. But it wasn't just
the scenery and the fine weather that made him feel good. He was
thrilled with himself for overcoming his fear on the bridge. After
their leap into the cool waters of the Otonabee they had swum
to the bank, and Lucy had laughingly applauded them. Wilson
had felt really proud of having done something so daring, and his
pleasure had been heightened when Lucy gave him the sketch she
had made of himself and Mike poised on the bridge.

He put a pinch of salt on his walleye and began to eat the fish. It tasted great, and somehow all the better for having been caught by their own efforts and cooked in the outdoors. Mike had brought along a bottle of home-made lemonade, and he poured the sparkling liquid into three battered enamel mugs that Wilson had borrowed from the school kitchen. They had chilled the bottle of lemonade in the shallow waters at the edge of the lake while preparing the fire, and the cool liquid tasted delicious as Wilson tipped back his mug and drank deeply.

He was about to return to his fish when they heard the sound of someone approaching along the shoreline trail. Looking up, Wilson saw a figure rounding the bend beside where they had set up their picnic.

'Hey, Taggart,' the boy said.

'Ledwidge,' answered Wilson.

Ricky Ledwidge was a slightly dim-witted boy a class ahead of Wilson. He was small but stockily built, and despite his plodding demeanour was a well-regarded hockey player who hung around a lot with his team-mate, the more forceful Moose Packham. Sure enough, Moose now rounded the bend, close on the heels of Ledwidge.

Wilson felt his heart sink, but he tried to sound unconcerned. 'Moose,' he said.

'Well, well, well, what have we got here?'

'Just having a picnic with friends.'

'Really?' said Moose, deliberately exaggerating his surprise. 'Didn't know you had friends, Taggart.'

'Well, he does,' said Mike.

Wilson was flattered that Mike had immediately stood by him, but all the same he hoped that Mike wouldn't antagonise Moose.

Moose didn't answer at once, but instead looked Mike and Lucy up and down as though appraising them, before turning to Ledwidge with a smirk.

'Old Taggart can really pick them, eh, Ricky?'

'Yeah, he can pick them all right!' answered Ledwidge.

Wilson could see the anger in Lucy's eyes, but to his relief she said nothing.

'What are you eating?' asked Moose.

'Just some walleye.'

'Stand up when you're talking to me, Taggart.'

Wilson hated being made little of, especially in front of Lucy, but he didn't want trouble with Moose Packham. He rose reluctantly.

'Walleye, eh?' said Moose. 'Do you know what? I'm feeling peckish. You feeling peckish, Ricky?'

'Yeah, very peckish, Moose.'

'How about you share your fish with us, Taggart?'

'You don't have to, Will,' said Mike, getting to his feet.

Moose turned to stare at Mike. 'I wasn't talking to you,' he said.

'There's a coincidence,' answered Mike. 'I wasn't talking to *you*. I was talking to my friend.'

Wilson couldn't help but admire Mike's coolness, even as he worried about how Moose would react to the unusual situation of someone defying him.

'Tell your new-found friend to mind his own business – if he knows what's good for him,' said Moose with quiet menace.

Wilson felt his stomach tightening, but he said nothing, not wanting to appear disloyal to Mike.

'No?' said Moose. 'OK, don't say you weren't warned. Now I think I'll have a bit of that fish,' he said, moving forward.

There was a sudden flash of sunlight on steel, and Lucy's Bowie knife embedded itself in the tree just above Moose's head. He jerked backwards in shock, and Lucy walked briskly forward, pulling the knife from the tree.

'Kinda jumpy, aren't you?' she said stepping back but holding Moose's gaze as she casually twirled the blade in her hand.

'You could have taken my eye out!' he said.

Lucy shrugged. 'That would still leave you with one eye.'

Wilson wanted to laugh but he knew that if he did he would pay later.

'Don't pick on Wilson,' said Mike. 'Lucy and I caught the fish, so they're not even his to give.'

Wilson prayed that Moose would let the matter drop, and for a moment nobody spoke.

'He can share his portion,' said Moose finally. 'When you gave it to him, it became his. And you'd like to share it with me, wouldn't you, Taggart?'

Wilson realised with despair that Moose was determined to humiliate him in front of his friends.

'Wouldn't you, Taggart?' Moose repeated.

'No, I don't think so,' Wilson found himself answering.

'Really? Found some guts, have you?'

Wilson felt his knees trembling, but he stood his ground.

'Maybe I'll take it anyway,' said Moose.

'I don't think so,' said Mike, who reached down and picked up the heavy wooden paddle of Lucy's canoe.

'Neither do I,' said Lucy.

'No? What do you think, Ricky?'

'Whatever you say, Moose.'

Wilson sensed that Ledwidge wasn't quite so bullish now, although he would still probably follow Moose's lead. But although Moose was bigger than Mike, and Ledwidge was bigger than him, Mike would be no pushover, and Lucy was still brandishing the Bowie knife.

Wilson realised that he needed to tip the balance by standing firmly with his friends. But what would happen back at the school when he hadn't got Mike and Lucy to back him up? Maybe he should just give Moose his fish. Then again if he did, he would be letting down Mike and Lucy, and Moose would continue to bully him in future. He breathed out deeply, then stepped over to stand beside Mike. He lowered his plate of fish to the ground and took up a thick stick from the woodland floor.

For a moment nobody spoke, then Moose laughed and shook his head. 'Keep your walleye. I'm not that desperate!'

Wilson felt a surge of triumph, knowing that Moose's laugh was phoney and that he wanted to back off without losing face.

'Let's go, Ricky,' he said. 'And we'll see you again, Taggart, when you haven't got your Guardian Angel there – and your little Redskin!'

Lucy reacted at once, the hand holding the knife quickly flicking forward. Moose and Ledwidge ducked to avoid the blade, then stood there foolishly on realising that Lucy was still holding the knife, and that this time she had simply pretended to throw it.

'Still kinda jumpy, aren't you?' she taunted.

Wilson couldn't hide a smile as Moose and Ledwidge sheepishly walked away, and although he knew that he might pay a price later, he felt elated at winning a victory with his friends.

CHAPTER TEN

Ciara thought that she would scream if the lawyer used the word 'aforesaid' once more. Why couldn't he use normal English like everyone else? Instead he had drawn up the paperwork about Granddad's estate, which referred to 'the party of the first part' – Ciara hadn't a clue what that meant. Dad caught Ciara's eye and winked, and despite the lawyer continuing to drone on, she smiled and gave Dad a quick wink in return.

They were seated in a high-ceilinged room in downtown Peterborough. The lawyer was a middle-aged man with horn-rimmed glasses, and thin lips that made him look disapproving. He was dressed in an old-fashioned suit and seated behind an old-fashioned mahogany desk – Ciara reckoned that he was the type to take pride in being old-fashioned about everything – and he seemed intent on dragging out the proceedings.

Earlier that morning Ciara had wished that Granddad had used a local lawyer in Lakefield, but when Dad had taken the scenic back road to Peterborough she had actually enjoyed the drive. The road skirted the river for most of the route, and she thought the Otonabee looked beautiful as its waters sparkled in the spring sunshine.

Now, though, she just wanted the lawyer to finish up and give her the letter from Granddad. At last the man reached the end of the document that he was reading, and he turned to Ciara, taking from his desk a sealed letter.

'Well, young lady,' he said, looking at her over the rim of his glasses, 'pursuant to your grandfather's stated wishes, it now falls to me to transfer this documentation to your custody.'

'Sorry?' said Ciara.

'This is the letter Granddad left you,' said Dad.

'The very last piece of paperwork – allowing us to conclude our consultation,' the man said as he handed the letter to Ciara.

'Thank you,' she answered, her excitement mounting.

Dad rose from his chair and shook hands with the lawyer, and Ciara followed his example. Then she made for the door, eager to leave the office behind and to discover at last what her grandfather wanted to tell her.

CHAPTER ELEVEN

Lucy watched the flames dancing against the evening sky. She liked the smell of burning wood. She liked too the contrast between the velvety blue of the dusk and the bright reds and yellows of the fire that burned cheerily at the meeting place in the centre of the reserve. Each evening people congregated here, strolling from the wooden houses to exchange gossip and catch up on the day's news.

Even though Lucy liked her independence – and especially her recent freedom to head off in her canoe – she also enjoyed the communal parts of Ojibwe life. Children were reared not just by their parents but also by aunts, grandmothers and the extended community, and food was frequently shared between neighbouring families. Just tonight Lucy and her mother had eaten fried venison, the meat taken from a deer that her friend Anne's father had hunted.

There was also a radio on the reserve now, owned by one of the more progressive families, and listened to by those members of the tribe who were interested in hearing the news, or popular music. Lucy loved the radio and tonight she had heard one of her favourite songs, 'Ain't She Sweet?' being played by a jazz band. Further west at Curve Lake, where her mother had grown up, Lucy knew there was even a brass band, but here at Otonabee there was no band. Some of the elders here frowned on modern music and were even against the presence of the radio.

Although Lucy disagreed with them, she sympathised with their desire to remain true to Ojibwe ways. She thought, however, that it made more sense to take pride in being Ojibwe, yet still to enjoy other parts of Canadian life, like art and music. But some people felt that they were at war with a government intent on wiping out Ojibwe traditions. They had a point, Lucy thought, with the government having banned many of the native ceremonies. Even pipe-smoking ceremonies had been forbidden, and Lucy had been told that the length of a traditional pipe had been reduced so that it could be hidden up a person's sleeve. She wasn't sure if this was really true, but there could be no doubting the government did want to end native customs.

Lucy looked about now and could see that her mother was chatting to other women at the far side of the fire, while most of the men were congregated on the side of the meeting place closest to the lake shore.

Lucy had arranged to meet Anne at the campfire tonight. Part of her wanted to tell Anne of this morning's confrontation with the bully from Wilson's school, and how they had sent him packing. But then she would have to explain about her friendship with Mike and Wilson. And what was the point of having a secret club if its existence was no longer a secret? And besides, Anne was a bit inward looking and probably wouldn't approve of Lucy making friends with boys from outside the tribe.

'*Aaniin*, Lucy,' said Anne now as she approached.

'*Aaniin*, Anne.'

'You missed the canoe-building.'

'I stayed out sketching longer than I planned.'

'Yeah?'

'If I'm to get a scholarship, I need to make the best portfolio I can.'

'Lucky you, getting off work to go drawing!'

Even though she said it with a smile, Lucy sensed that Anne was a little jealous – both of her talent, and of Mom giving her permission to go off and explore the lakes.

'Well, most days I do my art in the mornings, so I still help Mom with chores in the afternoon. And I collect lots of herbs when I'm travelling around.'

'Talking of travelling around – Harold Johnson said he spotted you up at Clear Lake.'

'Really?' Harold was a nosy boy of around her own age that Lucy had never really liked, and she hoped that he hadn't been spying on her. 'What was he doing at Clear Lake?'

'Delivering fish to a family with a holiday cottage there. He said he saw you with two white boys.'

Lucy was taken aback, but she kept her tone casual. 'They got a rope tangled round their rudder, and I used my knife to free it.'

'Yeah?'

'Yeah, and to pay me back they shared some fish they'd caught,' she added, deciding to keep her story as close to the

75

truth as possible, in case Harold Johnson had spied her eating with Wilson and Mike.

'Right.'

Lucy couldn't see Anne's face clearly in the flickering light from the fire, but it sounded as though Anne believed her. Lucy breathed a sigh of relief, then quickly changed the subject.

But she knew she could have been caught out. In future she would need to be more careful.

CHAPTER TWELVE

'I've a good one,' said Mike. 'Why did the belt go to jail?'

'Why?' asked Wilson.

'Because it held up a pair of pants!'

'That's silly!' said Lucy, but she was laughing as she said it, and Mike wasn't offended.

'OK,' he replied to her in playful challenge, 'you tell a better one.'

'Eh…why do birds fly south for the winter?'

'I don't know,' said Mike. 'Why?'

'It's easier than walking!'

Mike thought Lucy's joke was every bit as silly as his own but he still found it amusing. They were sitting in bright sunshine at the edge of the marsh to the west of Lakefield. Mike was cooking sausages on a small fire for their picnic lunch, and he looked over at Wilson now as the sausages sizzled in the pan. 'Your turn, Wilson.'

'Sorry. I don't know any jokes.'

'No?'

'Not really. But I know a riddle,' said Wilson hopefully. 'Will that do?'

'Yeah, riddles are great,' said Mike.

'So what's the riddle?' asked Lucy.

'What season is it when you're on a trampoline?'

'What season is it…' repeated Mike as he tried to figure out an answer.

'I know!' cried Lucy. 'Springtime!'

Wilson nodded. 'Spot on.'

Lucy grinned with delight, and Mike gave her a thumbs up. She was really smart, he realised. And brave too, he thought, recalling how she had supported him yesterday in standing up to Moose Packham.

Although today was only the third day that they had met up, already it felt like they had been friends for much longer.

Earlier this morning Wilson and Mike had sailed from the school jetty to the marsh, while Lucy had paddled to their rendezvous point in her birch bark canoe. Lucy had revealed that someone from the reserve had spotted them together yesterday, and she said that they needed to be more careful, to make sure that the G Club remained secret. Mike had readily agreed.

'OK, folks, muck in!' he said now, as he tipped the golden brown sausages from the pan onto an enamel plate.

'Muck in?' said Wilson.

'Don't tell me you never heard that before?' said Mike.

'No, actually.'

Mike laughed. 'You've had a sheltered life, Will! It means help yourself.'

Lucy had already chosen a sausage and was making herself a hotdog, using one of the bread rolls that Wilson had taken from the school kitchen. Mike and Wilson followed her example and they all sat back on the grassy verge at the edge of the marsh.

The day was warm, and a gentle breeze carried the scent of wild roses. For a moment nobody spoke as they savoured the summer heat and tucked into the food. Although the marsh wasn't that far from Lakefield it was off the beaten track, and Mike liked the sense of being in a hidden place. The high reeds bobbed and waved in the wind, giving glimpses of the sparkling waters of the backwater of the Otonabee that branched down to the marsh.

Earlier Lucy had captured the scene in a golden-hued water-colour that would be added to her portfolio. Mike thought that if there was any justice she must surely win the art scholarship. Unless of course she lost out because she was Ojibwe. It would be completely unfair if that happened, but Mike knew that some people were unfair when it came to dealing with Indians.

He looked at Lucy now. She was chewing her hotdog and sitting with her eyes closed and her face turned to the sun.

'You look like you're in a trance!' he said.

'Just thinking back,' said Lucy opening her eyes.

'Would you like to share your thoughts with the class?' said Wilson, imitating a school teacher.

Mike was pleased to see that the other boy had come out of his shell to the point of making jokes, but Lucy didn't smile, and instead looked a little wistful.

'I was thinking about my Dad. One of the first things I remember is food sizzling in a pan, and my Dad eating with me.'

'How old were you?' said Wilson.

'Maybe two and a half. So I'm not certain if I really remember it, or if it's a memory I have from Mom telling me about it. I like to think that it's a real memory of my Dad though.'

Mike nodded in understanding. 'And how are you so sure about your age?'

'Dad was home on leave from the war. He went back in September 1918, and he was killed in October.'

'I'm sorry, Lucy,' said Mike.

'Thanks. The sad thing is, the war ended just a month later.'

'That's awful,' said Wilson. 'To come that close to surviving.'

'I know. I think that's what Mom found hardest.'

'Is she still angry?' asked Mike.

'She's more sad than angry. But she knows he had to volunteer.'

Wilson looked surprised. 'Why did he have to volunteer?'

'Every man of military age on the reserve joined up.'

'But I thought the Ojibwe were kind of at odds with the government,' said Mike.

'We are. But the treaties we signed weren't with the Canadian Government – they were with the British Crown. And, once the Crown was at war, the Ojibwe men kept their word and came to its defence.'

'That's pretty noble,' said Wilson.

'Thank you.'

'So, where did your father die?'

'In Belgium. Near Neuve Chapelle.'

'My Dad fought in Belgium too,' said Mike.

'Yeah?'

'Yeah. He was a corporal in the Dublin Fusiliers.'

'At least he came back,' said Lucy. 'Not that I begrudge you. I'm really glad he came home in one piece.'

Mike thought of the nightmares that his father still endured, but he decided that was too private to tell the others. 'He came back in one piece but…well, some of the stuff that happened was awful. And Da's friend, Paddy O'Keefe, came back with half his face missing.'

'Gosh,' said Wilson. 'What did he do?'

'He couldn't bear people looking at him. And he hated wearing a mask. So he got a job as a cinema projectionist. It meant that, at work, he could stay in the dark.'

'That's really sad,' said Lucy.

'A lot of men who had bad injuries took that job.'

Lucy nodded. 'It makes sense, but it's still so sad.' She looked at Wilson. 'What about you, Will? We never asked about your Dad.'

Wilson put aside his hotdog, and Mike thought he looked slightly uncomfortable.

'Father wanted to serve, but he wasn't allowed.'

'Health reasons, was it?' asked Mike.

'No. No, his occupation was essential for the war effort.'

Lucy looked at him quizzically. 'What was he working at?'

'He was running the family's steel plant. They started making artillery pieces, and armoured cars, and later on they produced tanks and aeroplane parts.'

'That was important, sure enough,' said Lucy.

'Yes, they turned out a huge amount of stuff. Father's company...' Wilson looked uneasy. 'The company did really well out of it. It seems kind of wrong...'

'That's not your fault, Will,' said Mike. 'Or your Dad's. He was more valuable here than at the Front.'

'I suppose so. But compared to you two, it's not...very heroic.'

Mike shook his head. 'None of it was heroic, Will. My da talked about men being gassed, men being cut in two by shrapnel, men drowning in mud.'

'I'm sure you're right,' conceded Wilson. 'I was just thinking of the victory parades on the newsreels, and how proud the returning troops looked.'

'For all the good it did them. Da returned to Dublin to find out that he wasn't on the right side after all.'

Wilson looked confused. 'How do you mean?'

'There was an uprising against the British while Da was at the front. Irish people were fighting against the British to get their independence. So ex-soldiers like Da were treated like they had backed the wrong side.'

'I never thought of it that way,' said Wilson.

'I bet you never thought about how things were for the Ojibwe, either, after they fought,' said Lucy.

'No, what happened?'

'That's just it, nothing happened. Nothing changed. They came back to their reserves and were told that they couldn't vote, they couldn't do the native ceremonies, they couldn't leave without permission. They thought they'd have better lives after all their sacrifices. But they didn't, it's still the same now.'

'Gosh,' said Wilson, 'I feel like I've been sleepwalking. There's so much going on that I don't know about.'

Mike suddenly grinned. 'Hey, it's not your fault that you're rich! Anyway, let's cheer up and talk about something happier.'

'All right,' said Lucy. 'How about another sausage each and more jokes?'

'OK!' said Mike. 'What do you get when you cross a cat with a lemon?'

'What?'

'A sour puss!'

The others laughed, and Mike handed them each a sausage, then they sat back under a clear blue sky and basked in the growing heat.

* * *

Wilson sat in the school secretary's office, gazing at the telephone.

During term this was a busy place, but tonight the room was empty. Wilson had received permission from the headmaster, Dr Mackenzie, to take a trunk call from his father in America. The call was booked for eight in the evening, and Wilson had come down at half past seven, just in case the call came through early.

Sitting in the office with no adults present felt strangely exciting, as though he were trespassing, even though he had permission to be here. He had resisted the temptation to be nosy and to poke around in any of the drawers, but just sitting behind the desk and swivelling in the chair felt daring and enjoyable. The wall behind him was covered in photographs of school teams with boys holding trophies won at cricket, football and hockey. The other walls featured pupils from the cadet corps in army uniforms, and portraits of old boys from the school who had risen to prominence in various areas of Canadian life. Wilson had wondered if, some day, he might feature in one of these pictures. Certainly not for sport, but maybe if he were to become a leading pilot he could win recognition. Of course, Dad wanted him to go into the family business, but Wilson thought aviation was much more exciting than steel – although he hadn't yet said this to his father.

Wilson jumped as the telephone pealed loudly. He reached for it, eager to hear all the news from Cleveland, where Dad was still negotiating the takeover of an American company. He was half hoping that the negotiations might drag on, so that he could spend more time with his new friends. He felt a little guilty about it, but the G Club was great fun, and he had never before had friends like Lucy and Mike.

'Hello?' he said into the mouthpiece.

There was a click, then he heard the tinny sound of his father's voice.

'Hello, Wilson?'

'Yes.'

'It's Dad here.' Wilson suppressed a smile, thinking it would hardly be anyone else. 'How are you, son?'

'OK, thanks. And you?'

'I'm well. And I'm sorry that I've been delayed, Wilson. I presume you're managing all right?'

'Yes, I'm fine. I mean, I've missed you, of course, but it's been alright. I've made friends with a boy here, and we've done a lot of sailing.' Wilson felt bad about not mentioning Lucy, but he knew it was better to keep his friendship with an Ojibwe girl a secret from Dad.

'Glad to hear it. But I'm afraid I've bad news.'

'Oh?'

'This takeover down here, it's very important for our company. But it's been more complicated than expected. I'm afraid I have to stay in Cleveland a while longer.'

'OK, Dad, I understand,' said Wilson. He felt torn between disappointment and pleasure. Now there would be more time with Lucy and Mike.

'I'll make it up to you when I get to Lakefield.'

'How long more do you think you'll be?'

'Hard to say. The legal issues are proving tricky, but I can't walk away now.'

'No.'

'If things fall into place it could be just a few more days. If they don't, it could be a week or more. I'm sorry it's so up in the air, but I'll let you know when I've a better idea.'

'That's fine, Dad.'

'And I'll clear it with the school for you to stay on. I take it they're looking after you?'

'Yes, Cook lets me have first choice on everything she makes, so it's great,' Wilson answered cheerily, in a bid not to make his father feel bad.

'Right. And this boy you're friends with. Another pupil staying on, is he?'

'No, he's Mr Farrelly's son.'

'Mr Farrelly?'

'The janitor. He's married to Mrs Farrelly, the school nurse, and they live with their son Mike in the grounds.'

'Oh.'

'They're really nice people, Dad, they've had me to dinner twice.'

'Really?'

'Yes. And Mrs Farrelly is great fun. After dinner tonight she sang "Me and My Shadow". And she did all the actions with it, it was brilliant!'

'I dare say.'

Wilson felt disappointed at his father's lack of enthusiasm.

'The Farrellys, you said?'

'Yes.'

'Sounds Irish.'

'Yes, they came to Canada from Dublin about five years ago.'

'Sounds Catholic too. Are they?'

'Eh…I think so.'

'You think so?'

'It never really came up, Dad. But they had a Madonna and Child picture in their hallway, so I suppose they are. But Mike is great fun, and his parents are really nice.'

'I'm sure they're pleasant people, Wilson. And no doubt their intentions are good. But you need to be careful.'

'Careful of what, Dad?'

'The sons of gentlemen don't normally befriend the sons of janitors. I'm sorry if that sounds a little harsh, but that's how the world is.'

Wilson thought this wasn't just harsh – it was pure snobbery.

'I didn't befriend him, Dad, he befriended me,' he answered, unable to keep a hint of irritation from his tone. 'I was the one all alone, he has lots of other friends. He sees them in the afternoons, but in the mornings he's been decent enough to go sailing with me.'

'I've nothing against this boy personally, Wilson. I'm sure, as you say, he's perfectly decent and sound. And I'll commend the family to Dr Mackenzie for their hospitality to you.'

Wilson said nothing, sensing there was more to come, and that it wouldn't be good.

'But there's not just a class difference here. There's also religious belief.'

'But Dad–'

'Don't interrupt me, Wilson!'

'Sorry…I…sorry.'

'You're a Taggart, son. You come from a long line of proud, God-fearing Protestants. I'm not saying these Farrellys are bad people – but they're not *our* people.'

Wilson thought it was stupid to think you could only be friends with people who were the same as yourself, but he said nothing.

'You don't want to get too close to this boy and his family,' said his father. 'It's better for you, and it's better for them.'

Wilson felt like screaming, how is it better not to have Mike as a friend?! But if he argued too strongly his father might ban him from any contact with the Farrellys.

'Do you understand what I'm saying, Wilson?'

Wilson thought quickly. His father hadn't actually told him not to socialise with Mike and his family. Just not to get too close. So he'd stay friends with Mike, and not mention it again to Dad.

'Yes, I understand,' he answered quietly.

'Good. And I have some exciting news for you.'

'Yes?'

'One of the Americans we're dealing with has links to the aero industry. I told him you're a fan of Lindbergh, and he's going to try to get you a signed photograph.'

Normally Wilson would have been delighted with this news, and it was nice that his father was thinking of him. But Dad's attitude to the Farrellys had thrown him. He was determined to stay friends with Mike, however, and he knew it would be best not to give away how he really felt.

'Thanks, Dad, that's great,' he answered, brightly. 'So, what's Cleveland like as a city?' He sat back in the swivel chair and, as he listened to his father, he tried to keep his mixed emotions buried deep inside.

CHAPTER THIRTEEN

Ciara was stumped. The letter from her grandfather contained a series of clues that led to a secret manuscript – but the latest clue made no sense to her. Contained within the letter she had received from the solicitor was another small, sealed envelope that Granddad had called a 'safety net.' If Ciara couldn't get to the bottom of the clues that he had set then she could admit defeat and get directions to the manuscript's hiding place, via the sealed letter.

Ciara, however, was determined not to resort to this, even though some of the clues were tricky. She loved the fact that Granddad's sense of fun lived on, even after his death, and that their mutual fondness for riddles was getting one last outing. Now, though, she was perplexed as she sat in the spring sunshine in the large garden. The shadows on the sundial showed that the late afternoon sun was beginning to dip as she grappled with the hardest clue yet. She could have searched the internet for information on some of the clues, but she had made a deal with herself not to use technology. Instead she turned to her father.

'What's another word for a wide-barrelled weapon?' she asked.

Dad was sitting near her on an easy chair, sipping a coffee while reading the local newspaper.

'A cannon?' he answered, lowering the paper.

Ciara shook her head. 'No, it has to have eleven letters.'

'Ah. I guess that rules out "shotgun" as well.'

'It says "a wide-barrelled weapon (eleven letters)" will lead to a number I need.'

'OK…' said Dad, looking thoughtful. 'What about blunderbuss?'

'That's the gun that sort of opens out, isn't it?' said Ciara. She quickly counted on her fingers. 'And it has eleven letters! I bet that's it!'

'You and Granddad,' said her father with a laugh. 'You'd make a mystery out of striking a match!'

'Blunderbuss,' said Ciara, her mind racing. 'It rings a bell. Remember Granddad's story about the bus driver?'

'Yes…'

'Benny the Blunderer!' cried Ciara excitedly. 'That's what Granddad said they called him. He drove the bus into the Otona-bee River by mistake! Blunder – bus – it all makes sense!'

'Only if you've a warped mind,' said Dad with a grin. 'And how does a bus give you the number you need?'

'It was the number thirty-two bus. I remember saying to Grand-dad that it was the same number as our house. I'm sure that's the answer!'

'Maybe so,' conceded Dad.

'The clues I've cracked so far mean I have to be here in the back garden, and that I have to be looking west. I need to take another look at the verse.'

'Read it again,' said Dad.

Ciara shaded her eyes from the sun and read aloud.

Where to start and where to end?

That's the question, but pretend

You're a squirrel hiding food,

Would you seek the beasts that mooed?

Or would you rather show some sense,

Opting for what rhymes with dense?

High above or down below,

You must choose the way to go.

Start from where you see a face,

Then walk on at a steady pace.

Stop – a number tells you where.

You will know that you are there

When you see what you need most,

Something worn that rhymes with toast.

'The "beasts that mooed" are probably the cattle that were in that field for years,' said Dad, pointing.

'But Granddad says "Would you rather show some *sense*, opting for what rhymes with *dense*?" That means I probably should forget about the cattle – that it's more sensible to find something rhyming with dense.'

'What rhymes with dense? Tense? Pence?'

'They don't seem right,' said Ciara.

'Hence?'

She shook her head. 'Don't think so.'

'What else is there?'

'Fence!' said Ciara with sudden excitement. 'If you're looking west you've three choices. The field with the hedge where they kept the cattle, the field down by the stream, and the field that's cut off by the fence. It's the field with the fence!'

'Yeah, I'll buy that,' said Dad.

'High above or down below,' continued Ciara. 'There are trees in that field, so it could be hidden up in the branches. Or it could be buried at the base of one of them.'

'Start from where you see a face,' said Dad 'Could that mean starting from the study – where those sketches of Granddad are on the wall?'

'But if the number I need is thirty-two, I reckon that's thirty-two steps. And it's way more than that from the study to the fence.'

'Right.'

'What else has a face?' asked Ciara.

'A person? An animal? A clock?'

'But none of those would be in the garden all the time. Except...'

'What?'

'I have it! The sundial!'

'That's a type of clock right enough. And dial is slang for a person's face.'

'Is it?'

'Yes! That's the face you start from – the sundial!'

'OK,' said Ciara, 'let's try it!'

They both rose and swiftly crossed the lawn to the sundial.

'So I've to go thirty-two steps towards the field,' said Ciara.

'And what's the clue then?'

'Something worn that rhymes with toast.'

'Coast…boast…roast…'

'Most,' said Ciara, 'post…'

Suddenly they both looked at each other. The fence posts on the far side of the lawn were gnarled and worn-looking.

'That's it, Dad, that's it! I thought it was something you wore like clothing, but it isn't, it's something worn-looking!' cried Ciara. She pointed to the nearest fence. 'I bet you anything that thirty-two steps brings me to that old fence post over there.'

'I think you could be right.'

'And there's no tree overhanging it. So what we're looking for must be buried underneath the post.'

'Why don't I go get a spade?' said Dad. 'And you start counting out the steps!'

'Right,' said Ciara, 'let's dig for buried treasure!'

CHAPTER FOURTEEN

'Take your time, Lucy, it's not a race!'

'I know, but I want to finish this before I leave,' answered Lucy, her fingers moving quickly as she made mats with her mother at the kitchen table. The mats were made from birch bark, porcupine quills and sweet grass, and making them was a job she didn't like. She did it purely for the thirty-five cents they were paid for each dozen mats. It wasn't a lot of money, but the income mattered. With her mother a widow, and therefore only one adult wage coming into the home, Lucy knew that any contribution she made was useful.

Lucy worked skilfully now, a warm morning breeze flowing gently through the open window. Her mind drifted and she wondered what it would be like if her mother *had* remarried. Mom was thirty-three years old, and most Ojibwe widows of that age would have married again. Lucy was glad that Mom hadn't re-wed. Who knew what a step-father might be like, and she and her mother got on really well. On the other hand, maybe that was being selfish; if Mom met someone who made her happy, then she should be pleased for her.

Meanwhile, though, Lucy liked their independence and she admired the way her mother resisted pressure to conform to other people's wishes. She knew that lots of parents on the reserve

wouldn't have allowed their daughters to spend the summer painting and sketching, even if it was to try to win a scholarship. And
it wasn't just the older people who lacked enthusiasm for Lucy
studying to be an artist. Even her own friend Anne had asked her
what was the point in studying when she lived on a reserve. Lucy
had felt like asking why Anne assumed she would live all her life
at Otonabee, but had bitten her tongue instead.

'Where are you off to this morning?' her mother asked now.

'I might head up to Clear Lake. Maybe go as far as McCracken's
Landing.'

'Why don't you ask Anne or some of the other girls to go with
you for company?'

'No, I don't think so.'

Her mother look surprised, and Lucy realised that she had
spoken too emphatically. 'It's just…it's less distracting if I'm on my
own. I can concentrate more on what I'm painting.'

'Whatever you prefer, love,' said Mom.

Lucy felt guilty about misleading her. But she couldn't say that
she was seeing Mike and Wilson without revealing how they had
already been meeting each morning. Better to change the subject.

'Can we go to hear the brass band at Curve Lake soon?' she asked.

Her mother liked visiting her old home and nodded agreeably.

'All right. Maybe we'll travel over on Sunday?' she suggested.

'Great. I'm dying to hear them do 'Ol' Man River.''

'What's that?'

'It's a hit song from a new musical. Anne says she heard them
playing it, and it was brilliant.'

Her mother smiled at her. 'Well, if Anne says it's brilliant, we'd better get over there!'

Lucy felt a sudden surge of affection for her mother and she reached out and squeezed her arm. 'Thanks, Mom, you're the best!' She rose from the table. 'Right, that's that done!'

'One other thing, love. I need you to do something for me.'

'Of course.'

'Will you keep an eye out for some woundwort.'

Lucy's mother was a skilful herbalist whose potions were used to treat a wide range of ailments at Otonabee.

'I'll scour the countryside till I find some! See you later.'

''Bye, Lucy. Go carefully.'

Lucy kissed her mother's cheek, and gathered her bag of art materials and her picnic lunch.

Outside the sky was blue and the birds were singing from the treetops. It was another glorious morning as she headed off along the woodland trail towards where the canoes were beached. She was looking forward to today – she wanted to tell Mike about a fiddle that she had heard.

Suddenly a man's voice rang out.

'Hey, girl!'

It was the Indian Agent, Mr Staunton. Lucy turned and faced him, forcing herself to look polite and interested. He drew near and stared at her accusingly.

'What happened to my fish the other day?'

'Nothing happened to it. I didn't–'

'You didn't bring that bass to my office,' he interrupted, 'even though I told you to. Offered you good money, too.'

'I didn't catch any.'

'You spent the day fishing and caught nothing?'

'I didn't say I caught nothing.'

'So you did catch some.'

'I didn't catch any bass. That's what you asked me for.'

'Don't get smart with me, girl!'

'I'm not getting smart, Mr Staunton. Just telling you what happened.'

'What did you catch?'

'I caught walleye.'

'Why didn't you bring me that instead?'

Lucy felt like screaming. Why should she bring anything to such a rude man? And why should he consider it as his right? She struggled to keep her patience.

'Because you didn't say you wanted walleye.'

Staunton drew nearer and looked at her aggressively

'You watch that mouth of yours, missy,' he said.

Why don't you watch your own? she longed to say. But even though Staunton was unreasonable, he represented the government. If she stood up to him there would be trouble. He could probably make sure that she didn't get awarded the art scholarship. Hating herself for doing so, she forced herself to sound meek.

'I'm sorry there was a misunderstanding,' she said. 'And the next time I'm fishing, I'll bring you some of the catch, whatever it is.'

He stared at her for a moment, as though deciding whether or not this was satisfactory. 'Do that,' he said curtly. 'Right, be on your way then.'

Lucy nodded in farewell, then stamped on, keeping her anger hidden as best she could. Some day I'll be independent and successful, she fumed, and then I'll show him – and all the other Stauntons of this world!

As she left the Indian Agent behind and strode through the sweet-smelling pines towards where her canoe was beached on the shore, she felt a little better. She quickly launched the canoe, then paddled away at speed, working off the rest of her frustration on the sparkling blue waters of Lake Katchewanooka.

Wilson felt a sinking feeling in his stomach as he sat on the edge of his bed. He had known that he might pay a price for defying Moose Packham and Ricky Ledwidge, and now the moment of truth had arrived. It was two days since the incident at the bridge, and Wilson had been hoping that the more time that elapsed, the less significant the incident might seem to the other boys. But now one look at Moose's face told him otherwise.

'If it isn't Taggart the Tough Guy,' said Moose, blocking the door to Wilson's dormitory cubicle. 'But then again – maybe you won't be so tough without your gang to back you.'

Wilson swallowed hard and rose from the bed, trying not to let his fear show.

'Look, it was a needless conflict to begin with,' he said. 'Why don't we just forget it?'

'A 'needless conflict', eh? Very fancy with the words, aren't you, Taggart?' said Moose, drawing closer.

Wilson's instinct was to back away but he forced himself to stand his ground. The morning sunlight shone in through the dormitory window and in the bright light he could see Moose's chest and shoulder muscles bulging under his tight-fitting tee-shirt.

'Very fancy with the words for two reasons, I reckon,' said Moose. 'One, you blab a lot because you're too yellow to fight.'

Wilson didn't respond, and Moose drew even closer.

' And two, you think it makes you sound smart, as if you're not stuck up enough!'

'Stuck up?'

'Yeah.'

'Your father takes the biggest villa in Lakefield for the summer, but you think *I'm* stuck up?'

'I don't like posh people who look down their noses.'

'I never looked down my nose at you. Or anyone else. And if being posh is a crime, every boy in this school is guilty.'

'There you go again, Taggart. Twisting words to defend yourself. Well, I've news for you. Ask me what the news is.'

Wilson hesitated, and Moose's face darkened in irritation. 'Ask me what the news is!'

'What's the news?'

'Talk won't save you! That's the news!' laughed Moose, and he suddenly reached out and pushed Wilson in the chest.

Wilson staggered backwards but managed to remain on his feet.

'You were cock-of-the-walk when you had your knife-throwing savage around,' said Moose with a sneer, 'and your big, thick janitor's son.'

'Lucy's not a savage, and Mike isn't thick!'

'They're savage and thick if I say they are! And there's no-one to save you now, Taggart, no teachers in the dorms, no other boys whose fathers have abandoned them.'

That stung Wilson, but he was desperately trying to think how he might escape from this situation. His eyes swivelled from the door to the window.

'It's just you and me, Taggart, 'cause unlike you, I don't need help to fight my battles. I fight my own fights and leave my friends out of it.'

Wilson made a move towards the door, but Moose raised a hand in warning.

'Don't even think of running! The only thing you have to decide is, are you going to beg for mercy, like the whipped pup you are? Or are you going to fight? Your choice, Taggart – what's it to be?'

'Hey, Ma,' said Mike, 'why did the man with one hand cross the road?'

'I just know this will be silly.'

'To get to the second-hand shop!'

'Mike, that's terrible!' said his mother. But she was laughing as she said it and Mike's father couldn't help but smile, even as he shook his head.

'Where do you get these jokes?'

'In the junior page of the newspaper.'

Mike knew that if he wanted to persuade his parents to do something it was important to ask them when they were in good humour. He had sensed that the time might be right this morning. For a treat, Ma had done flapjacks and maple syrup, and when they had cleared away the breakfast things, she had spread on the table a brochure from the White Star Shipping line.

In the five years since the family had emigrated to Canada they had never been back to Ireland. Now, though, his parents were hoping that by saving hard they might pay for a family trip to Dublin the following summer. Mike loved the idea of meeting all his cousins again. He knew too that his parents still missed their relations, despite being happily settled in Lakefield, and that they were excited about the prospect of a holiday in Ireland.

The atmosphere was good now, and Mike decided the time was right to ask his question.

'You know how we're celebrating Dominion Day next Sunday?' he said.

'Yes?' answered Ma.

'Could Wilson join us for the day, and maybe stay here that night instead of going back to the dormitory on his own?'

Mike looked appealingly to his parents. He sensed that Ma was agreeable to the suggestion, but she looked to his father before responding. Mike tried to gauge Da's reaction. He suspected that he was torn between doing a hospitable thing and his notion that Wilson was too different from them.

'There'd be no awkwardness, Da. He needn't join us until we're back from Mass and he's finished at his church.'

His father considered this, then nodded.

'All right, he can join us for the day. But I don't think he should stay overnight.'

'Ah, Da!'

'He's a nice boy, Mike, I know that. But I'm sure his home is a lot fancier than ours.'

'I'll have you know, Thomas Farrelly, that there's nothing wrong with our home!' said Ma with mock indignation.

Mike was glad to see his mother taking his side and he sensed that his father was weakening. 'Please, Da, it would be horrible to celebrate the day together and then send him back on his own to the dormitory.'

'He could share with Mike for one night,' suggested Ma. 'I can make up Patrick's old bed.'

Da looked at both of them then smiled wryly. 'I'll never get a minute's rest till I agree. All right, he can stay on Sunday night. But only Sunday night. We're not running a guest house!'

'Thanks, Da! Thanks, Ma!'

'Go on with you,' said his mother with a wink.

'See you later,' said Mike as he left the kitchen and stepped out into the warmth of the June morning. It was going to be another scorcher, he thought, as he made his way through the grounds of the school. He passed the open space that was used as an ice rink in the winter. Today the contrast was striking as a warm breeze lightly buffeted a group of coloured butterflies that hovered in the air. Mike continued on his way, happy that he had secured his parents' agreement about Wilson, and warmed by the sun.

Just as he reached the entrance to the dormitories, he heard a cry in the distance. He paused, thrown. The voice sounded like Wilson's voice. Was he in trouble? Mike moved quickly towards the sound. As he reached Wilson's end of the corridor he heard another cry – much more clearly this time – and the voice of his friend shouting 'No!'

Mike burst in the door to the cubicle as Wilson screamed 'Let me go!'

He had been expecting to find a thief, but instead he saw Moose Packham viciously twisting Wilson's arm behind his back. Wilson was clearly in pain and his face was covered in a sheen of sweat.

'Let him go!' cried Mike.

A look of anger crossed Moose's face as his eyes fell on him.

'You again!' he said, keeping his grip on Wilson as he glared at Mike. 'I'm tired of seeing you.'

'Just let him go!'

'Mind your own goddamn business, Farrelly!'

Mike was taken aback at the use of his name but before he could respond, Moose continued.

'Oh yeah, I know your name all right – know you're just a jumped-up janitor's son, too! You're not a pupil here. You've no right to be in this building. So get the hell out of it before I give you a hiding, too!'

Mike felt his heart pounding. The other boy was bigger and stronger than him but he knew that he mustn't show fear.

'I don't walk away when my friends are in trouble,' he said.

'Your funeral, pal.'

'Please,' said Wilson, 'can we just–'

'Shut up, Taggart!' snapped Moose, forcing Wilson's arm even further up his back.

Wilson shrieked in pain, and Mike took a step forward. Moose pushed Wilson down onto his bed and, in one swift movement grabbed a canoe paddle that was resting against the wall and swung it. Mike ducked, the wooden paddle missing his face by inches. Moose, thrown off balance by the miss, regained his footing and swung the paddle again. This time he changed tack and instead of aiming for Mike's face he went for the body. The cubicle was small, which didn't leave Mike much room to manoeuvre, but his reflexes were fast. He jerked back and the paddle didn't connect properly, instead scraping along his chest.

Mike glanced around, seeking some weapon with which to defend himself. Nothing was to hand, though, and already Moose was gripping the paddle, wearing a humourless smile, ready to deliver another blow.

'Should have run when you had the chance,' he said, as he swung back the paddle to strike again.

Mike balanced on the balls of his feet, ready to dodge the blow. But it never came. From the bed Wilson reached out and grabbed the tip of the paddle, at the end point of Moose's backswing. He clung onto the paddle and kicked out wildly, catching Moose at the back of his knee.

Moose cried out in pain and anger, then rounded on Wilson. It meant taking his eye off Mike for a moment, and Mike instantly reacted. As Moose swivelled round toward Wilson, Mike leaped forward. He grabbed the paddle that Wilson had loosened from Moose's grip and he drove it forward like a battering ram, catching Moose squarely in the stomach with the handle. The bigger boy cried out in agony and collapsed onto the bed, badly winded. Wilson rolled away from him and got shakily to his feet.

Mike immediately moved in on his opponent and raised the paddle.

'No!' cried Moose, barely able to get the word out as he gasped for air.

Mike had no intention of clubbing someone who was helpless, but he needed to frighten the bully, and this was his chance. He made as though to bring the club down, and once more Moose gasped 'No!'

Mike kept the paddle raised. 'Lay off Wilson in future. Do you hear?'

Moose panted and nodded.

'I said, 'do you hear?''

'Yes!'

Mike held the paddle threateningly for another moment, then

lowered it. 'Now get out of here before I change my mind.'

Moose was still clutching his stomach but he seemed to be getting his breath back, and he managed to get to his feet awkwardly and shuffle to the door. He turned the handle and opened it, then stopped. With his left hand holding his stomach, he slowly turned around and pointed with his right finger at Mike. His breathing was laboured but his words dripped with venom.

'You'll pay for this, Farrelly,' he croaked.

'I'm quaking in my boots,' answered Mike coolly, even though his knees were actually trembling and his heart racing.

'You shouldn't even be in college buildings. You're trespassing here.'

'He's not trespassing, he's my guest,' said Wilson, who was now standing shoulder to shoulder with Mike.

'Non-pupils aren't allowed into the dorms, Taggart! And he's no pupil – he's a nobody, the son of a workman.'

'You're as thick as a plank, Packham,' said Mike angrily. 'You pick on Wilson because you claim he looks down on you. But then you look down on me because my father is a workman. So you're a hypocrite, as well as being a snob yourself. And you're too stupid to even see it.'

'We'll see who's stupid. Maybe your father won't be a workman much longer. Maybe Dr Mackenzie won't keep a man whose son attacked a pupil with a canoe paddle.'

Mike hadn't expected this. Suddenly he felt sick.

'Don't worry, Mike, that won't happen,' said Wilson.

'We'll see about that,' said Moose.

'Think it through, Packham,' said Wilson. 'You'd be a real hero, wouldn't you, if everyone heard you'd been beaten by a younger boy – and then you squealed and tried to have his father sacked.'

'You shut your stupid mouth, Taggart!' said Moose.

Mike raised the paddle again and Moose backed off into the corridor, still bent over in pain. 'This isn't over,' he said, jabbing his stubby finger at the boys. 'Not by a long shot!'

He turned and limped away.

Wilson turned to Mike. 'He nearly broke my arm! Thanks for saving me.'

'Thanks for saving *me*. You grabbed that paddle just at the right time.' Mike tried for a grin, but he was worried about Moose's threats and it ended up more like a grimace.

As though reading his mind Wilson laid a hand on his shoulder. 'I promise you, Mike. What he said – that's not going to happen.'

Mike wanted to believe him. But supposing Moose's father did go to Dr Mackenzie? The headmaster was decent and fair, but maybe he would feel he had to side with a parent whose son had been assaulted on school property by a non-pupil. And if Dad lost his job, not only could they forget about visiting family in Ireland, they would lose their cottage too, and be homeless.

'He said all that to try and save face, Mike. And even if his father *did* go to the Head, I'd tell them what really happened. OK?'

'OK,' answered Mike, relieved at Wilson's response, and grateful for his support, but still worried for his father's job.

CHAPTER FIFTEEN

Ciara's excitement mounted as she heard the spade striking something solid. Bathed in golden light by the late afternoon sun, her father had been digging up the earth around the fence post, and now he stopped and looked expectantly at Ciara.

'I bet that's it, Dad,' she cried. 'Keep digging!'

He shifted more soil, then there was a metallic thud as the spade struck the solid object again. He widened the hole that he had been making, then slipped the spade beneath a rectangular shape that had emerged.

'It's some kind of box,' said Ciara.

Her father jerked the spade upwards with his wrist, and a mud-covered, rusty box came clear from the earth.

Ciara dropped to her knees. She reached for the box, not caring if she got her hands muddied, and she placed it gently on the grass.

'It's a strongbox,' said Dad. 'There should be a clip to unlock it.'

Ciara ran her hands over the box, the earth moist to her touch. There was a clasp at the front and, although it was dirty and rusty, it sprang open when she pressed it. She could feel her heart thumping and she looked up at her father, his frame silhouetted by the golden sunlight.

'I'm almost afraid to open it, Dad.'

'Why?'

'I'm dying to know what's in it. But another part of me is afraid that…I don't know…maybe I'm going to find out something scary.'

Her father dropped down to his hunkers and placed a hand on her shoulders. 'Granddad wanted to share this with you, Ciara. If it was something you shouldn't know, he would never have done all this. You meant the world to him.'

'I suppose so.' Ciara could feel her nervousness draining away to be replaced by excitement.

'So… time to finally solve the mystery,' said Dad.

Ciara nodded. 'Yeah,' she said, then she lifted the lid and opened the box.

CHAPTER SIXTEEN

Lucy sighed in frustration, then with several deft brush strokes she covered over the section of her painting that wasn't right. A couple of days previously she had woken early and risen to see a magical combination of soft white mist and the pink glow of dawn over Lake Katchewanooka. Now she was painting in bright sunshine on Webster Island and trying to recreate with oils the scene that she had captured in her mind's eye.

She was pleased with the way she had caught the ghostly looking mist, and at how the light blue of the skyline was tinged with pink from the rising sun. But the reflection of the tree line in the waters of the lake somehow hadn't been right, and she was glad that she had resisted the temptation to let a minor detail pass uncorrected.

She wiped her brush, then considered how to proceed. Every painting she did mattered, and she had to make each one as perfect as possible if her portfolio was to win her the scholarship. Sometimes she had doubts about whether or not she was talented enough to succeed. But Mom always told her to believe in herself, and most of the time she could dismiss her doubts and channel her energy into trying harder.

She desperately wanted the scholarship. She knew that no other job would fulfil her as much as being an artist. She was also honest enough to recognise that it would be a form of escape. In many ways she liked Ojibwe life, but she found it restrictive to live on a reserve, and she hated being controlled by someone like the Indian Agent, Mr Staunton. Since the incident regarding the fish, she had brought him a couple of bass that she caught in the lake. In fairness he had paid her, as promised, but she still disliked his overbearing attitude, and she resented the fact that every person at Otonabee was answerable to him, even the elders.

Mike and Wilson, by contrast, were free to live as they pleased. Lucy had never before had friends outside the tribe, and she was intrigued by the difference in how white people conducted their lives. But despite their differences, in some ways she felt closer to Mike and Wilson than she did to Anne, whom she had known all through her childhood. Perhaps it was the bonding effect of having a secret club. Or maybe it was the fact that Anne never seemed to want to change anything, whereas Mike and Wilson had open minds. They were interested in music, and the craze for aviation, and Wilson was fascinated with history. And both of them were really encouraging about her painting and sketching.

She wasn't foolish enough to think that their lives were perfect. It seemed sad to Lucy that Wilson's wealthy father would leave him in the school during summer holidays. And though Mike lived in the grounds of The Grove, he couldn't attend as a pupil.

She found Wilson to be more low key than Mike, more reflective and cautious, whereas Mike was the adventurous and impulsive one, and more outgoing, with his jokes and riddles. The combination of all their personalities seemed to make for a really good mix.

But though they were having a great summer together she wondered what the future held for their friendship. Could it have *any* future, given their different backgrounds? She really hoped so, even though it would be tricky, and many people would be against them.

Her musings were cut short by the sounds of approaching footsteps. Lucy looked up and smiled as Mike and Wilson rounded the bend in the trail leading to the glade that was their rendezvous point.

'*Aaniin*, Lucy!' they said.

'*Aaniin*, boys.'

'Gosh, great painting!' said Mike.

'I love the way you've caught the light!' said Wilson. 'And the mist – really spooky!'

'Thanks,' said Lucy, 'you're good for my confidence.'

The boys lowered their picnic gear to the ground, then flopped down onto the grass.

'So, any news?' said Lucy.

Wilson nodded. 'Yes, actually.'

'What?'

'Moose Packham tried to get revenge on me for the other day. And Mike really gave him his come-uppance!'

Lucy decided that her painting could wait a few minutes, and she put down her brush, then turned to Mike. 'OK,' she said, 'Tell me all about it!'

* * *

The noon-day sun beat down from a cloudless sky, and Wilson moaned in mock despair as Mike took out his book of riddles.

'Mercy!' cried Wilson, 'it's too hot to scramble our brains!'

Even though they were in the shade of a large pine tree on the edge of the glade, the heat made for a drowsy, relaxed atmosphere. Wilson was glad that they hadn't travelled far today. While Lucy had finished her oil painting, followed by a charcoal sketch of the glade, the boys had sunbathed and played checkers. Mike was a good player, but Wilson had a slight edge, and he had taken pleasure in beating his more athletic friend. Now Mike had put away the portable set of checkers and taken the book of riddles from his rucksack.

'Riddles are good for your brain!' he said. 'Here's a good one – what has one foot, one head and four legs?'

'Is this a joke one, or does it make sense?' asked Wilson.

'It makes perfect sense.'

'One foot, one head and four legs...' repeated Lucy, her brow knotted in concentration.

Despite his mock protest, Wilson was curious now. 'Is it some kind of animal?'

'That would be telling.'

'How about a one-legged man on a horse?' suggested Lucy.

'Not bad,' said Mike. 'But not right either. Will I tell you?'

'Give us a clue, instead,' said Lucy.

113

'You have to leave it every morning.'

'One head, one foot, four legs…and you leave it in the morning,' mused Wilson.

'I know!' cried Lucy. 'It's a bed!'

Now that he knew the answer, Wilson was disappointed that he hadn't figured it out, although in fairness, Lucy had been very quick.

'Give the girl a cigar!' said Mike playfully.

'Yuck,' she answered. 'Who'd want a horrible, smelly cigar!'

'Well, what would you like as a prize?'

'Eh…how about this whole island? Then it could be our private playground.'

'You don't want much, do you?' said Mike.

'It *would* be great to have our own island,' said Wilson, 'like you read about in adventure stories. Pity that Webster Island is someone's private property.'

'It wasn't always,' said Lucy quietly.

'How do you mean?'

'When this was Ojibwe land, it didn't belong to one individual.'

'No, I suppose not,' said Mike.

'To be fair,' said Wilson, 'once the Crown signed treaties with the tribes, they had to give the land to individuals. Or settlers would never have come.'

Lucy looked Wilson in the eye. 'Do you know the history of that?'

'Yeah. I've been working on my family tree. Some of my family came from the Bann Valley in Ireland to Ontario to settle land.'

'Did you know that lots of early settlers would never have survived their first winter if it weren't for the tribes? We showed them how to build against the cold, the places where the lakes wouldn't freeze, where they could fish, where they could trap. We could have let them starve and freeze to death, but we didn't.'

'My family didn't come with the really early settlers, so it didn't happen to them, but all you've said is true. It says a lot about the Ojibwe and the other tribes.'

'We got no thanks for it, though. They just took our land, and more and more settlers came.'

'That sounds really unfair,' said Mike.

Wilson held up his hand in a gesture of surrender. 'It was unfair, I'm not saying it wasn't. But all through history people have moved from one place to another.'

'If they moved from one part of Ireland to another it would make sense,' answered Lucy. 'But coming all the way to Canada?'

'People with a sense of adventure will sail a long way.'

'Adventure? So your people weren't coming here to escape the potato famine?'

'No, that happened earlier. My grandfather was the younger son on a big estate. He came to Canada to seek his fortune.'

'And you're going to The Grove School, so he succeeded.'

Wilson felt a bit uncomfortable and it must have shown, because now Lucy raised her hand in a gesture of appeasement. 'I'm not saying any of this is against you, Will, you're my friend, and none of it is your fault. But every new arrival took away land that had been used by tribal people.'

Wilson could see that Lucy and Mike were looking to him for a response, and he hesitated. He didn't want to fall out with Lucy, but if they were going to stay friends it had to be based on honesty, and he wouldn't be true to himself if he didn't say what was on his mind.

He gathered his thoughts, then spoke in a reasonable tone.

'You said every new arrival took someone's place. But that's just human history. People have always moved, and every group who settled anyplace were arrivals once. Every Canadian was an arrival at some stage, Lucy. French, British, Irish, German – we all started off as arrivals.'

'Not the Ojibwe. This was our land first.'

Wilson knew that he had to tread carefully here, and he made sure not to make his voice sound argumentative.

'Not really, Lucy. After meeting you I went to the school library to learn more about the Ojibwe. They've been here a long while. But that's because way back in time they drove out the Huron tribe. So even the Ojibwe were arrivals at one point.'

Wilson could see that Lucy was taken aback.

'I'm not trying to be smart,' he said gently, 'It's just the way the world is. It's changing all the time. The best we can do is go with the change and try to be as fair as possible.'

Lucy looked thoughtful.

'Maybe,' she answered. 'And I'm not trying to be smart either.

But it's easier to go with the change if you're white, and rich and powerful, isn't it?'

'Well…well, yes, I suppose so,' admitted Wilson.

'Imagine seeing the change through the eyes of someone who's not white, someone who's poor and powerless. Have you ever done that?'

Wilson hadn't been expecting this line of questioning, but he answered honestly. 'No, I haven't.'

'Maybe you should. Because here's the question, Will. Would you still go with the change then?'

Wilson didn't answer at once, and Lucy held his gaze.

'Didn't think so,' she said.

CHAPTER SEVENTEEN

'Was it hard for you and Da to get jobs when you came to Canada?' asked Mike, trying to keep his enquiry casual-sounding. His father had gone to work, and Mike was helping Ma to clear away the breakfast things from the kitchen table. A day had passed since Moose Packham had made his threat about Da losing his job. So far nothing had happened, and Mike had the promise of Wilson's support if Moose did lodge a complaint, but he still felt uneasy.

'It wasn't that hard to get work,' she answered. 'But it was hard to get two jobs in the same place. We were very lucky to both get taken on in The Grove.'

Mike nodded, even though this wasn't what he had hoped to hear.

'Why do you ask?' said Ma.

'Oh…it's just…Wilson was doing a project about his family tree. When they came to Canada, how they got started – all that stuff.'

'Right.'

Although Mike's query had arisen because of Moose, he was curious about the family leaving Dublin, and he thought this might be the moment to find out more. 'Wilson had loads of information, and… and I was wondering…'

'Wondering what?'

'Well, about our family. We never really talk about coming to Canada.'

'There's not much to talk about. Times were tough in Ireland, so we came here to make a fresh start.'

Mike remembered a conversation he had overheard between his brother, Patrick and his sister, Edith, and he looked enquiringly at his mother. 'But…well, wasn't it also to do with Da fighting in the Great War?'

His mother hesitated, and Mike knew he had touched on something sensitive. Da rarely spoke of his experiences as a soldier, and there was an unwritten family rule that nobody ever referred to the fact that Da sometimes had nightmares about the war, and woke screaming.

'As you know, Da fought in the British Army,' answered Ma carefully. 'While he was at the Front, the rebels rose up in Ireland against the British in 1916 – the year you were born. When the rebels eventually won the War of Independence, men like Da were seen as being in the wrong camp.'

'That's so unfair. I mean, those soldiers really suffered, and they thought they were doing their duty.'

'Life often is unfair, Mike.'

'And was Da picked on, because he'd served?'

'It wouldn't be true to say he was picked on. But men like your da were treated like…like they were an embarrassment. In the new Ireland, no-one wanted to hear their war stories. No-one wanted to hear about their sacrifice – even though tens of thousands of them died.'

'That's awful.'

'It is. But at the same time it's…it's kind of understandable too.'

'How is it?'

'The Irish Free State was just starting out as a new country, Mike. The people running it didn't want anything to do with the British Empire. And men like Da were a reminder. So ex-servicemen learnt to keep their heads down – it's just the way things were.'

'But Da wasn't prepared to keep his head down?'

Ma looked at Mike and to his surprise she gave him a wan smile. 'You mustn't set Da up on a pedestal, love. He was a brave man, who fought for what he thought was right at the time. But after the Great War he'd had enough of fighting to last a lifetime. So to answer your question, he kept his head down – like all the others.'

'Right.'

'Money was scarce in Ireland, and so was work. And then to end up on what people saw as the wrong side – it made things tough. Canada offered opportunities, so we came here. Does that make sense?'

Mike nodded. 'Yes. Yes, of course.'

'Better not to bother Da with any of this though. He's put it behind him now. All right?'

'Yes, I …I won't say anything.'

'Good lad. So, where are you and Wilson off to this morning?'

'We're going swimming up past Young's Point.'

'Well, enjoy yourselves, and be careful.'

'Thanks, Ma, we will.' Mike gathered his packed lunch from

the table, then kissed his mother on the cheek and headed for the door.

He thought that Da should have been treated better after what he endured in the trenches, and he felt offended on his behalf. Most of all though he thought that his father didn't deserve any more trouble, and he hoped, yet again, that the fight with Moose Packham wouldn't come back to haunt them.

'So – what do you *never* do if you come across a bear?' asked Lucy, as the three friends had their picnic lunch on the grassy shoreline of Clear Lake.

'You never run away,' said Mike, 'They just catch you, they're too fast.'

'But I heard somewhere you should run *downhill* if you meet a grizzly,' said Wilson.

Lucy shook her head. 'That's a myth. Bears can charge at thirty miles an hour– you won't outrun them.'

Wilson gave a sheepish grin. 'Guess I've just proved I'm a city slicker.'

Lucy smiled. 'Don't worry, we'll make you a country boy!'

Wilson was pleased that she was joking with him. He had been a little worried after they parted yesterday. He feared that Lucy might have mulled over what he said about the Ojibwe displacing the Huron from their land and taken offence. He had considered too her comment that it was easy for his family to be philosophical about changes when they were white, wealthy and powerful.

Today, though, Lucy had shown no coolness, and the matter hadn't been mentioned again. Wilson was relieved, as he had grown to like her a lot, as well as being fascinated by her insights into tribal life – not to mention bear encounters.

'So what else don't you do if you meet a bear?' she said.

'You don't get between them and their young,' answered Mike.

'And you don't stare them in the eye,' added Lucy.

Wilson had never heard that before. 'Why not?'

'It's like a challenge to the bear,' explained Lucy.

'So, what should you do?'

'What you should really do is avoid meeting a bear in the first place,' she answered.

'By making noise to warn them off – even I know that much,' said Wilson.

'But also looking out for signs they might be around.'

'What kind of signs?' he asked.

'Claw marks in mud, droppings, scratch marks on trees, ravens gathering at a kill site.'

'Right.'

'Last summer I actually came across a grizzly.'

'Yeah?' said Mike.

Lucy nodded. 'He came out of a belt of trees about fifty yards away. I knew at once he'd seen me.'

Wilson was intrigued. 'What did you do?'

'I stopped dead. Then I spoke in a calm voice, and slowly raised my hands over my head.'

Wilson looked at her quizzically. 'What does that do?'

'Raising your hands makes you seem bigger and less vulnerable. And talking let's the bear know you're human. Lots of times they'll back off then.'

'And did he back off?' said Mike.

'No. Maybe there were cubs nearby, who knows? Before I could back away he suddenly charged me.'

'No! You must have been scared stiff!' said Wilson.

'I can't really remember – survival took over.'

'What did you do?' queried Mike

'Climbed a tree to get out of his reach. I never climbed so fast in my life!'

'But bears can climb,' said Wilson.

'Black bears can, but grizzlies are poor climbers. After a while, he lost interest and left.'

'How long did you stay in the tree?' asked Mike.

'Quite a while. I didn't want to take any chances.'

'I would have stayed there for the rest of the day!' said Wilson.

The others laughed, then there was a companionable silence as they all tucked into their lunches once more.

Wilson felt the warmth of the sun on his face and he sat back chewing a toffee bar and savouring a sense of wellbeing. Earlier they had had a swimming race and he was pleased at having beaten Lucy and Mike. There was a big emphasis on sport in The Grove

School, but Wilson wasn't sporty. He had never shone at hockey, or cricket or football – which affected his standing with his classmates. The one physical activity he was good at was swimming, and he valued the respect that he had won from Mike and Lucy.

It was funny how things turned out, he mused. He had begun the week tagging along with Mike, but now it felt like all three of them were equals. There was something really nice about that. He wished that he could write to his father and tell him about their adventures. But Dad would be angry, and besides, part of what made the G Club so enjoyable was the fact that it was secret. Better to say nothing and just let things take their course, he decided. He chewed on his toffee, closed his eyes and lay back happily on the sweet-smelling grass.

CHAPTER EIGHTEEN

Ciara felt her pulse quickening as she opened the heavy brown envelope that had been inside the buried box. She was sitting in her grandfather's study, with a desk lamp illuminating the gloom now that the light outside was fading.

Dad had obviously recognised that this was a special moment for her, and she appreciated that he had left her to experience it in private. Normally Ciara shared the events in her life with Mam, and with her friends back in Dublin, but tonight she hadn't gone on Facebook and hadn't texted anyone. Somehow it felt like this was just between herself and Granddad.

She paused, half nervous, half excited by the prospect of what she might discover. Then she took out a manuscript from the envelope. She had thought that Granddad might have used an old-fashioned typewriter, but the manuscript, bound together with treasury tags, had perfectly even lettering. Granddad had printed it from a computer, so it must have been written in recent years.

The manuscript was quite thick, and Ciara realised with pleasure that she had a long read ahead of her. First though, there was a single, loose sheet of paper, and Ciara turned it over and started reading.

Dear Ciara,

Taking a human life is truly a huge step. Its consequences can affect people for the rest of their lives. To understand any situation, however, requires knowing the background, which is why this account has been written. Normally life and death decisions on justice take place in a court of law. That didn't happen here, for reasons that will emerge. But before anyone passes judgement they need the full facts, and so, now that all involved are dead, finally the facts can be revealed.

Ciara put down the sheet of paper and sat unmoving for a moment. What had happened – and who had died – all those years ago? she wondered. Then she sat forward, took up her grand-father's manuscript and began reading.

CHAPTER NINETEEN

'I think Harold Johnson really likes you,' said Anne to Lucy. It was evening at Otonabee and they were strolling towards where the sun was setting behind the gathering place.

It's a pity I don't like Harold then, thought Lucy, but she bit her lip. It had been an enjoyable day. She had paddled all the way to Stony Lake this morning, had some fun with Mike and Wilson, and then painted a picture that she reckoned was one of her best yet. She was relaxed, so now she kept her tone casual as she replied to her friend.

'What makes you think he likes me?'

'He asks about you a lot. I bet he'd like you as a sweetheart.'

'Forget that!' said Lucy. She got on well with most of the boys on the reserve and she had grown really friendly with Mike and Wilson, but she wasn't interested in having a sweetheart or even talking about boys, the way Anne was.

'Lots of girls think he's handsome,' Anne continued. 'And everyone says he's going to be a very good hunter.'

'Let some other girl be his sweetheart then – 'cause he needn't start hunting me!'

Anne smiled at the retort. Lucy sensed that her friend was a little in awe of Harold, but Lucy had never been keen on him.

127

They had even had a minor clash when he had suggested that she should concentrate on the type of stone art that the Ojibwe had traditionally engaged in, rather than 'painting for white people', as he described her oil colours on canvas. How could he believe that someone who had such different values from him, would want to be his sweetheart? Assuming, of course, that Anne was right, and not just letting her imagination run away with her.

Lucy kept her thoughts to herself, and, as the two girls walked along the trail, the sound of rhythmic drumming carried on the breeze. Up ahead Lucy could see the flames from the bonfire, with sparks rising into the air over the clearing where people gathered in the evenings. Anne stopped and put her arm warningly on Lucy's.

'Look, Mr Staunton is talking to your mother.'

Lucy looked ahead, and sure enough Mom was in conversation with the Indian Agent.

'I hope everything is all right.' said Anne.

'Why wouldn't it be?'

'I don't know. But you don't want to get on the wrong side of Mr Staunton.'

Lucy didn't like the way Anne was so fearful in these situations and she decided not to be intimidated.

'Let's walk up and join them,' she said.

'Are you sure?'

'We haven't done anything wrong, Anne, and I'm sure Mom hasn't either.'

Before her friend could object Lucy resumed walking. Anne joined her, although Lucy could sense her unease. But if people went around in fear of the Indian Agent when they had done nothing wrong, weren't they just playing into his hands, and making him even more powerful?

The two girls came abreast of Lucy's mother and Staunton, and Lucy greeted them politely. Mom returned her greeting, and the Indian Agent gave a brusque nod then continued his conversation.

'You want permission to visit Curve Lake?' he said

'Yes,' answered Mom. 'And these are the two girls I intend to bring with me.'

'You intend to bring? I haven't given you permission yet.'

'Well, that's why I stopped and asked you.'

Lucy admired the way her mother wasn't awed by Staunton the way some of the other adults were. At the same time she was keeping her tone reasonable, and Lucy realised that she was following her own advice. Mom had always told her to avoid conflict when she could, and if possible to try to get results without turning everything into a challenge.

'Why do you want to go there?' asked Staunton.

'To visit relations.'

Staunton considered this then turned and pointed at Anne. 'She's not part of your family, is she?'

'No, she's Lucy's friend.'

'Then she wouldn't be visiting relations.'

Lucy saw Anne swallowing nervously, even though she wasn't

guilty of anything. She didn't know why Staunton was acting this way – other than the fact that he enjoyed wielding power.

'Anne wouldn't be coming to meet her relations, but she would meet mine,' answered Ma, her tone polite but not pleading. 'She'd also be coming to hear the brass band.'

Staunton turned and looked again at Anne.

'Music lover, are you?' he asked sarcastically.

Lucy could see that Anne was frightened, and she answered instead.

'We both love music, Mr Staunton. Just as much as you love bass,' she added.

Staunton gave her a searching look, and Lucy tried to keep her face impassive. She didn't know what had prompted her to make the remark about the fish. Staunton's behaviour had been mean, and Lucy resented having to ask permission to travel off the reserve, so maybe that had made her react. She wondered if Staunton might think she was trying to win him over, in reminding him of the bass she had delivered to him. On the other hand, he might take it as a veiled threat that, if he messed them up any more, his supply of bass might dry up.

He stared at her for a long moment, as though unsure how to respond, then he nodded. 'All right then, you can go.'

'Thank you,' said Mom, but already Staunton had turned away.

Lucy stuck her tongue out at his retreating form. She saw her mother stifle a giggle. She winked at Mom, then joined arms with her and Anne and continued towards the bonfire.

* * *

Wilson licked his melting ice cream, not wanting to lose a drop as he crossed the main street of Lakefield. The sun had just set, and he could see the fiery sky reflected on the waters of the Otonabee River as he cut down Burnham Street towards the water's edge.

Every Saturday night he used some of his pocket money to treat himself to a strawberry cone and now he felt relaxed as he made towards the river, savouring the taste. He could hear a piano playing in a nearby house and the sound of a woman singing 'Oft in the Stilly Night.' Wilson paused. It was a song his Great Uncle Samuel in Northern Ireland liked to perform, and its haunting melody transported Wilson back to the previous summer.

He and Dad had sailed across the Atlantic to spend their holidays on the old family estate near Kilrea in County Derry. At a party one evening Uncle Samuel had stood rigidly at the piano, singing in a strong baritone voice, as his daughter, Wilson's Aunt Charlotte, accompanied him. It was an old Irish tune, and Wilson wondered idly if tonight's singer might be an Irish woman. He knew that lots of Irish immigrants had settled in this part of Ontario, although as a pupil in The Grove he didn't have a great deal of contact with local people.

Still, it was a link to the old country, and the memories of the holiday with Dad made him feel slightly wistful as he reached the water's edge and looked out over the river.

The roaring of the Otonabee was deafening as it cascaded though the sluice gate near the bridge at the top of Main Street. Wilson thought of what an adventure it would be to travel all the way from Lake Huron to Lake Ontario along the waterway. Maybe he and Dad could do some of that journey next year for their summer holiday – he might suggest it in the letter he planned to write to his father later.

Wilson sucked in a large dollop of ice cream and began to walk along the riverbank, mentally rehearsing what he would say in his letter. The conversation with Lucy about the Ojibwe and the early settlers was fresh in his mind, but he would have to be careful. He would love to find out more about his grandfather's experiences when he had come to Canada as a settler in the late 1860s. Grandfather had made his fortune in steel, but he had started off in farming. Had he had dealings with the Ojibwe, or with other tribes? And was the original family homestead on the Cobourg Peninsula built on what had previously been Indian land?

If Wilson asked any of those questions, however, his father would want to know what had prompted them. And he couldn't tell Dad about Lucy – he would never approve of their friendship. Even writing about the Farrellys was going to be tricky, considering Dad's previous reaction. But then again, not to refer to them at all would surely sound suspicious too.

Wilson stopped near where the train track ran on a spur line to the steamer jetty. He looked out across The Narrows, where the water coming from Lake Katchewanooka speeded the flow of the

Otonabee. The sky had a beautiful crimson tinge, but Wilson was distracted from the scene by his calculations.

His father had clearly told him not to get too involved with the Farrellys. But Mrs Farrelly had invited him to join the family for dinner tomorrow to celebrate Dominion Day. And Mike had been such a great friend, fearlessly defending him from Moose Packham. Was he really supposed to turn his back on Mike and his family just because Dad didn't approve of them being Catholics?

Wilson didn't like being deceitful, and Dad had always maintained that it was important to be honest in your dealings, whether in business or in private life. But although Dad was right about most things, Wilson knew he was wrong about the Farrellys.

He stared unseeing across The Narrows, then turned away, his mind made up. He had accepted Mrs Farrelly's kind invitation and, come what may, he wasn't going to go back on that, even though it meant deceiving Dad. Satisfied with his decision, he popped the last part of the cone into his mouth, turned away from the water's edge and started back towards The Grove.

CHAPTER TWENTY

Mike sat at the dinner table biding his time. It was three days now since Moose Packham had made his threat about Da's job, and so far nothing had happened. But Mike believed in the old saying 'know your enemy', and he wanted to know – without being too obvious – about the Packhams and their Maple Brewery in Peterborough.

Edith and Patrick, Mike's sister and brother, lived and worked in Peterborough and had taken the early morning train back to Lakefield to be with the family for Dominion Day. Because the national day had fallen on a Sunday this year all five members of the family had gone to Mass together. Later they had been joined by Wilson, who had attended a church service in the Anglican chapel in the school grounds.

Mike had been hoping that his brother and sister would like his new friend, and to his relief they had, so that now the atmosphere at the dinner table was relaxed and light-hearted. Wilson had got things off to a good start by arriving with flowers for Ma and a packet of tobacco for Da to thank them for having him as a guest.

Although Wilson was wealthy and had a generous allowance Mike still felt it was a thoughtful gesture. He sensed too that his father had warmed a bit more towards Wilson, despite Da's earlier reservations about the difference in class and religion.

Mike still thought it was silly to put too much emphasis on someone's religion, although part of him could see why Da felt the need to be loyally Catholic in a predominantly Protestant town. But the whole community celebrating together on Dominion Day had been unifying. There had been music and speeches, a regatta on the water, and a funfair with booths and rides, and stalls selling food and drink. Best of all, there had been a feeling of optimism about the celebrations, a sense that Canada was a place where everyone could have a promising future, and for a while Mike had forgotten his worry about Mr Packham getting Da fired from his job.

Now, though, Edith and Patrick had begun to talk about work opportunities in Peterborough, and Mike sensed his chance. Finishing off his blueberry pie, he pushed aside his bowl. He caught his sister's eye and tried to keep his tone casual.

'So what about Maple Brewery, is that a good place to work?'

'Not if you're a typist,' answered Edith. 'Martha Barnes works there.'

'Who's she?'

'A girl I know from French classes. She said they drive you pretty hard and the money is only OK.'

'Yeah, I heard that they're not a great employer,' said Patrick. 'Why do you ask?'

'There's a boy in the school here whose father owns the brewery. Wilson knows him too,' said Mike.

'George Packham,' said Wilson. 'They call him Moose.'

'Moose? I take it he's a bit of a bruiser?' suggested Patrick.

Wilson nodded. 'You could say that.'

'I've patched him up in the infirmary once or twice after football matches,' said Ma. 'He strikes me as the type who gives as good as he gets.'

Mike and Wilson exchanged quick glances, but before either one could respond, Patrick laughed. 'Sounds like a chip off the old block then.'

'How do you mean?' asked Da.

'The rumour in Peterborough is that the owner of Maple Brewery does more that just brewing,' answered Patrick.

'More, as in...?' queried Ma.

'As in smuggling liquor. Rum-running across the border into the States.'

Mike knew that although they had relaxed the liquor laws here in Ontario, the prohibition of alcohol sales was still in place in the United States. It meant that gangsters from America were importing alcohol that was made legally in Canada. It was said to be a shady, dangerous business and it wasn't reassuring to think that Moose had a father who had power in this violent world.

'There's plenty of smuggling goes on,' said Da. 'And, now you mention him, I think I know this Moose lad. Is he a heavy-set boy with wavy fair hair? Bit of a swagger?'

Mike was glad that his father had noted Moose's unappealing cockiness, but he let Wilson answer the question.

'Yes,' said Wilson wryly, 'that would be a good description of him.'

'The family have rented a place on the lake for the summer,' said Ma. 'I saw the mother in the butcher's yesterday.'

'Really?' said Edith. 'Does she look like a gangster's moll?'

Ma was amused. 'Let's say she doesn't look like she'd be joining the sewing circle. But she must like having guests. She was buying masses of meat for a Dominion Day barbeque.'

'That's where you should have gone, Will,' said Patrick. 'Instead of eating with the boring, law-abiding Farrellys, you could have been rubbing shoulders with gangsters and rum-runners!'

Wilson smiled. 'I'm much happier here, thanks all the same.'

'Did he invite you?' asked Edith. 'This Moose boy?'

'No, he doesn't like me.'

'Really? Why not?'

'Edith. You mustn't quiz our guest!' said Da.

'It's all right, Mr Farrelly, I don't mind,' said Wilson politely.

Mike was watching closely, and his friend gave him a conspiratorial wink. Mike wasn't sure what Wilson was at, but he guessed that he might be taking the chance to lay out the facts against Moose.

'He's not a very nice person,' said Wilson. 'He's friendly with Ricky Ledwidge and a few others, but most boys are wary of him.'

'Don't mess with The Moose?' said Patrick.

Although the comment was said lightly, Wilson answered it seriously. 'That's exactly how he wants people to feel – scared of him. He doesn't like me because he thinks my family are higher up the ladder than his.'

'And are they?' asked Edith.

'Edith!' said Ma.

'Well, let's say my Dad doesn't have to smuggle rum for a living!'

Everybody laughed, and Mike was pleased at how well Wilson was making his case. With any luck it would never come to it, but if the Packhams tried to have Da dismissed Wilson could be a good witness for the Farrellys.

'Anyway Moose is a bully and a numbskull,' added Wilson. 'He'd never have asked me to his barbeque, and I wouldn't have gone if he had. But I'm really glad you invited me here, so thanks again.'

'You're more than welcome,' said Ma. 'And now, after we clear away the dishes – what time will it be?'

'Eh, about six-thirty,' answered Wilson.

'Right answer, but also wrong answer!' said Ma playfully. 'What time is it, family?'

'It's party time!' cried Mike, Patrick and Edith, in what was an old family joke.

'I hope you have a party piece, Wilson,' said Ma.

'Well…'

'Because no-one escapes!'

'Ma knows all the Percy French songs,' explained Mike. 'And even Da belts out 'Roses are Shining in Picardy' – like a crow!'

Da pretended to be offended, and Wilson laughed aloud. Mike felt relaxed, and he smiled at his friend, glad that he had invited him, and happy to put aside for now his worries about Moose Packham.

* * *

Lucy listened a little distractedly as the Curve Lake Brass Band played 'One Alone' from the popular musical *The Desert Song*. It was a beautiful tune, and Lucy loved hearing the band playing, yet she felt dissatisfied.

She had travelled with Anne and her mother to Mom's old home at Curve Lake Reserve. It was always fun to meet up with aunts, uncles and cousins, and the extended family had eaten their fill of grilled venison and squirrel on the sunny shores of Chemong Lake.

The band wasn't a novelty to the family members who lived at Curve Lake, however, and so Lucy, Mom and Anne had left the others to go and hear the musicians, who were playing in the centre of the reserve. It should have been a carefree afternoon, but Lucy was feeling increasingly frustrated with Anne.

They had known each other since childhood, but lately Lucy couldn't help but feel that she had outgrown her friend. In contrast to Lucy, Anne never wanted to embrace change, never wanted to challenge old ways of doing things. Of course, you couldn't expect your friends to be exactly the same as you, but Lucy was finding that they had less and less in common. And instead of being excited and encouraging when Lucy got the chance of the art scholarship, Anne had been lukewarm and in some ways even discouraging. Only this morning she had said Lucy shouldn't get her hopes up too high about winning, and that in the long run she might be happier just living on the reserve. It wasn't meant maliciously, but Lucy still resented Anne's attitude and found herself wondering what sort of a friend would want to hold you back.

Part of the problem, she realised, was that meeting Wilson and Mike had broadened her horizons. The boys were interesting, and funny, and had been enthusiastic about her art right from the first meeting. Even though there was no possibility of joining them for the Dominion Day celebration in Lakefield, she knew if they *had* been together there would have been more fun than she was having with Anne.

'I'm not mad about that song,' said Anne now, rising from the grassy mound on which they were sitting. 'Excuse me for a bit.'

'OK. You know where to go?' asked her mother, indicating the direction to the toilets.

'Yes,' said Anne, 'back in a minute.'

Lucy watched her friend walk away, then she thought that this might be a good time to ask her mother about something that had been bothering her.

'Mom?'

'Yes, love?'

'You know the way it's Ojibwe land at Otonabee, and here at Curve Lake?'

'Yes.'

'Was it always our land?'

Her mother looked slightly surprised at the question. 'It's been ours for generations. Ojibwe settled here in 1829, so there's 'no-one on the reserve who can remember living anywhere else.'

'But back before that, did the Ojibwe clash with some other tribe and take their land?'

'Well, lots of tribes clashed in the old days. There were wars over fur and trading. Some tribes fought on the side of the French against other tribes, some with the English. The Ojibwe fought the Iroquois, the Huron, the Winnebago.'

'So we would have taken this area from someone else?' said Lucy.

'Yes, way back in time the Huron settled this region.'

'Right.' So Wilson had been correct.

'Why do you ask?'

'Just…just something I heard somewhere. I didn't really know what the history was.'

'In those day it wasn't written down. The stories were passed from generation to generation by word of mouth.' Her mother looked at her quizzically. 'You've never been all that interested in history before.'

'I was just…just curious about it…'

Lucy sensed that Mom wasn't entirely convinced by her answer, and it was time for a diversion. 'I love this tune!' she cried, as the band played 'I'm Looking over a Four Leaf Clover'. 'It's got a great beat, hasn't it?'

'Yes, I suppose it has.'

'And here's Anne.'

Lucy turned away a little and watched as her friend approached, relieved that Mom wasn't pressing any further. The band was playing the tune as a march, and Anne tried for a playful salute. Lucy saluted back, but Anne's playfulness looked awkward and forced. It brought home to Lucy how natural the fun was when she was with Wilson and Mike. She wished that they could openly be friends, though she knew that was impossible.

She settled back on the grass, listening to the music and looking forward to tomorrow – and the next meeting of the G Club.

CHAPTER TWENTY-ONE

Ciara sat propped up in bed, fighting to keep her eyes open. It was half past ten at night, but because of the time difference between Canada and Ireland it was now the middle of the night according to her body clock. Despite her tiredness, she was gripped by the contents of her grandfather's manuscript. It was fascinating to see the world through the eyes of Granddad as a twelve-year-old, and she turned another page, eager to learn more of his adventures in the summer of 1928.

Her reading was interrupted by a knock on the bedroom door, then Dad put his head around the door.

'Hi, Dad,' said Ciara, lowering the manuscript.

'Hi, honey.' Her father crossed the room and sat on the side of the bed. 'Just came in to say good night.'

'OK.'

'So,' said Dad, indicating the manuscript. 'Solved the mystery yet?'

'Not yet. All I know is that somebody dies. But I don't know who, I haven't got to that part.'

'So what have you read?'

'All about the summer when Granddad was twelve. He formed a secret club with two other kids.'

'A secret club?'

'Yeah. The girl, Lucy, was Ojibwe, and the boys were white, so

143

they all felt they had to keep it a secret from their parents.'

Dad nodded. 'We've made progress since then, but that's how things were in the past.'

'And when you were growing up in Lakefield, Dad, did you ever meet Wilson or Lucy?'

'No. I heard their names mentioned now and again, but I never met either of them.'

'If I read on for a bit I could find out what happened.'

'I think you'd be better off getting some sleep.'

'Ah, Dad!'

'Come on, Ciara. You've flown enough to know the drill. The way to handle jet lag is to try and sleep at bedtime in the country you've arrived in.'

'I know, but I'm dying to find out what happens.'

'You'll know soon enough.'

'I suppose. It's really interesting though to read about Granddad, and how he got on with his mam and dad. Can you remember them?'

Her father shook his head a little sadly. 'Afraid not. My grand-parents died within a couple of years of each other – just before I was born.'

'Shame. But even though he kept it a secret about his friends, Granddad seemed to get on well with his mam and dad.'

'So I'd always heard.'

'Did you get on well with Granddad when you were a kid?'

'Sure I did.'

'What did you do together?'

'Lots of things. He taught me to sail, and to ice skate. Why do you ask?'

Ciara hesitated, fearful that she might hurt her father's feelings. 'It's just…well, it seems this manuscript is really important. I wondered why he didn't leave it to you.'

Dad gave her a gentle smile and reached out and squeezed her hand. 'It's OK, Ciara, I don't see it as some kind of snub. Granddad and I got on fine, but remember, I left Canada when I was twenty. I came to Dublin to go to college, and, as you know, I met Mam and I've lived in Ireland ever since. So I never really spent much time with Granddad, adult to adult.'

'Right.'

'And then you came along. And you're so like him in personality that you've always been his pet.' Dad grinned 'I can't say it in front of Connor or Sarah, but you're a chip off the old block, and you were the favourite grandchild.'

'Connor and Sarah weren't into the puzzles and all.'

'Exactly. And neither was I. So Granddad probably thought – leave this to Ciara, she'll enjoy all the preamble of finding it, but then, once you'd read it, he'd know you'd pass it on to me. So he was killing two birds with the one stone.'

'Well…that's OK then,' said Ciara. 'But you must be still dying to know what happened?'

'Of course,' said Dad. 'But Granddad waited ninety years to tell the story. I think we can wait another day.'

'All right,' conceded Ciara, as she reached out and placed the manuscript on the bedside table.

''Night, Honey,' said Dad, kissing her on the cheek.

''Night, Dad.'

Her father left the room and Ciara switched off the light and lay down in bed. Her eyes felt heavy and she suddenly realised just how tired she was. But the events of 1928 occupied her mind, and so she yawned and stretched, eager to get sleep out of the way, and to resume reading the story of Granddad's past.

CHAPTER TWENTY-TWO

Wilson's mind was secretly racing as he worked alongside Mike. It was the morning after Dominion Day, and with other boys from the Lakefield area they were helping with a clean-up after yesterday's celebrations. There had been fireworks, musical performances and fairground attractions on an open space beside the river, and now the volunteers were working in hazy sunshine, picking up litter, sweeping pathways and generally restoring the riverside area to its normal tidiness.

Wilson had really enjoyed his Dominion Day dinner with the Farrellys, and had even sung 'It's a Long Way to Tipperary' when encouraged to do a party piece. He wasn't a very good singer, but the Farrellys applauded him heartily, and he had basked in the warm, relaxed atmosphere.

But that had been last night, and now he feared that he had undone some of that goodwill. During the night Wilson had been awoken by shouting from Mike's parents' room. Mr Farrelly had been screaming about a gas attack, and Wilson had heard Mrs Farrelly saying 'It's all right, Tom, it's all right'. After that, things had quietened down again. He didn't know if Mike had been woken too, but not wanting to embarrass his friend, Wilson had pretended to be asleep.

From what Mr Farrelly had been shouting, Wilson realised that he was having a nightmare about his war experiences. Even though it was almost ten years since the Great War had ended, Wilson knew that countless veterans still carried scars, both physical and mental, from the horrors of that conflict. Eventually Wilson had gone back to sleep, but the strange environment meant that he slept a little fitfully, and he had risen early while the others were still in bed.

Going into the kitchen, Wilson had been surprised to see Mike's dad.

'Mr Farrelly,' he said. 'Sorry, I didn't know you were up.'

'I woke early. No point tossing and turning.'

Wilson thought that maybe this was Mr Farrelly's way of referring to the nightmare. He felt that he ought to say something in response.

'Everything…everything OK now?'

'Why wouldn't it be?'

'Just…well, lots of people have bad dreams,' said Wilson gently.

'Sorry?'

'My uncle served in Flanders. He still dreams about mustard gas attacks.'

Wilson wanted only to ease any embarrassment Mr Farrelly might be feeling. Instead the man's face seemed to harden as he looked Wilson in the eye.

'What are you trying to say, son?'

'Just that…that lots of people have bad memories of the war. That it's nothing to be…' Wilson had been going to say it was nothing to be ashamed of, but he realised from Mr Farrelly's expression that he had misjudged things badly in referring to the nightmare at all. 'Just that lots of brave men suffered,' he concluded.

'Right.' Mr Farrelly nodded, then went briskly through the kitchen door.

Wilson could have kicked himself. He had enjoyed a wonderful day with the Farrellys and now he had gone and insulted his friend's dad.

That had been several hours earlier, but Wilson still felt embarrassed. He hoped he hadn't hurt Mr Farrelly's feelings too much and, on a more selfish note, hoped that it wouldn't prevent him from spending time with the family in future.

'Uh-oh,' said Mike now. 'Look who's appeared.'

Wilson followed Mike's gaze and saw Moose Packham and Ricky Ledwidge arriving to help with the clean up.

'Good timing,' joked Wilson, 'now that most of the work is done.'

But Mike's face was serious. Wilson realised the reason when he saw that the other two boys were approaching.

'Well if it's not the Bobbsey twins,' said Moose with a sneer.

'If it's not Tweedledee and Tweedledum – with the emphasis on dumb,' retorted Mike.

Wilson was impressed by Mike's quick wit and cool demeanour, even though he knew his friend was still worried by Moose and his threats.

'You have a really big mouth,' said Moose.

'Yeah, you need to shut that big mouth,' said Ricky.

Mike turned to Wilson. 'Can you hear an echo here, Will? Or is it just some half-wit repeating what his leader says?'

Ricky's eyes narrowed in anger, but it was Moose who responded. 'You think you're so smart – you thick, Irish Paddy!'

'Not that good at English, are you?' said Mike. 'You can say someone is thick, or smart, but not thick and smart. That's called a contradiction.'

Wilson felt that he should support his friend. 'And as for an Irish Paddy – I don't think there's any other kind, is there?'

Moose didn't have an immediate answer. Instead he pointed a stubby finger into Wilson's face. 'You'll pay for this, Taggart.'

Wilson felt a chill, knowing that this was probably true. But he had learnt from Mike, who maintained that showing weakness before a bully only encouraged him, so he held the other boy's gaze.

'If I do, maybe you'll pay a bigger price,' he answered, pleased at his own daring. He wasn't sure what his answer meant, but it sounded good, and he could see that Moose was a bit taken aback.

Moose then turned to Mike. 'And don't think I've forgotten. Trespassing in the dormitory and assaulting a pupil with a weapon.'

Mike didn't change his expression, but Wilson knew he would be concerned about Moose's threat regarding his father's job.

'Come on, Ricky, let's leave these deadbeats to it,' said Moose. He turned back to Mike. 'Do a bit more cleaning up there, Farrelly. It'll be good practice for the kind of job you'll have when you grow up.'

Ricky laughed, then the two boys walked off.

'Don't worry, Mike. If he lodges a complaint I'll give the other side of what happened.'

'Thanks, Will,' Mike said, and nodded as though that were the end of the matter.

Wilson sensed that he was putting on a brave face, and as they went back to work he wasn't sure who exactly had come out on top – he and Mike, or Ricky and Moose.

Part Three

Departures

CHAPTER TWENTY-THREE

Lucy hid her canoe. She tied it firmly to a tree stump at the edge of Lake Katchewanooka, carefully camouflaging it with over-hanging shrubbery. Only the most careful search would uncover it now, and she was confident that it wouldn't be spotted while she carried out her mission.

The early afternoon sun shone brightly, and Lucy moved away from the water's edge. She had learnt the basics of hunting and tracking on the reserve, and she stepped carefully so as not to make any sound as she made her way along the trail that wound through the Packham estate.

She had spent an enjoyable morning with Mike and Wilson, and they had swapped tales of how they had spent Dominion Day. Lucy had then done some painting, there had been the usual jokes and riddles, and they had eaten their picnic lunch before the boys sailed back to The Grove. It had been great to see Mike and Wilson, and they had agreed to meet again at Webster Island the following day.

Now, though, Lucy was taking a risk. She was trespassing on the estate that Moose Packham's father had rented for the summer. Lucy had taken an instant dislike to Moose, a dislike that had deepened when she heard about his further bullying behaviour. There was nothing she could do to make him less obnoxious to

Mike and Wilson, but she had come up with a mischievous idea that she thought would amuse her friends.

Her plan was to sneak through the estate until she came in sight of the house. Once there she would sketch the building, using the charcoal stick and paper that she had in her pocket. She would then add a comic caricature of both Moose and his friend Ricky, and draw exaggerated versions of their heads poking out through windows of the house. She reckoned that the combination of making fun of their enemies in the drawings, and her entering the Packham estate, would impress Mike and Wilson.

She walked along the wooded lakeside trail, avoiding snapping twigs or disturbing the shrubbery. She could smell wild garlic on the hot summer air, and even though she was nervous, she also felt excited and alive.

Turning a bend, Lucy came to an old wooden boathouse with a jetty. A metal bridge, which swung aside when boats were launched, allowed her to continue along the trail, but she stopped and listened carefully. No sounds came from within. She advanced cautiously.

To the rear of the boathouse there was a mud track, and to the front the trail continued along the shoreline. There was a heavy wooden door, but the timber was rotted and it was slightly ajar. Lucy poked her head inside. The boathouse was quite large, with a shady interior, and there was nobody there. There were no boats in storage either, but lots of wooden crates, with the name of Packham's Maple Brewery stencilled on their sides.

Relieved that there was no-one around, Lucy continued along the trail. She knew that another few minutes' walk would bring her to the gardens surrounding the house itself, at which point she would need to be really vigilant. Still, if she stayed hidden in woodland she could quickly sketch the building and then add the caricatures later. She pictured in her mind's eye both Moose and Ricky, and considered which of the features of each boy she could best exaggerate for comic effect.

Suddenly her musings were banished. There were voices. She stopped dead. She heard the voices again, louder this time. It sounded like two men, and they were coming her way.

Lucy knew from talking to Mike and Wilson that, although Mr Packham dressed like a dandy, he was big and tough-looking. And if a man was walking the trail on this estate, there was a good chance that it was Mr Packham.

Lucy's mouth went dry, and she stood as if frozen. Then she heard the voices again, closer now, and her fear spurred her into action. She turned and ran silently back in the direction of the boathouse. She tried not to panic, and she forced herself to slow down, watching what she was stepping on underfoot.

Back at the boathouse, the rotted wooden door was sufficiently ajar for her to squeeze in. She paused, trying to decide what to do. She could hide here, or risk running back out along the trail. Running would take her away, but if the men heard her they might give chase and catch her before she could untie her canoe and escape.

She weighed things up for a second or two, then she followed her instincts and quickly squeezed through the door, and into the gloom of the boathouse.

The rain lashed against the window pane of the school secretary's office, and Wilson looked out at the deluge, grateful that the bad weather hadn't spoiled Dominion Day by coming a day earlier. It was eight in the evening now and still light, but the heavy grey clouds made the vista outside the window look dull and depressing. Wilson felt warm and dry as the breeze buffeted the window frame. The raindrops splattered against the glass, then ran down the window pane as though racing each other.

The sudden change in the weather had caught him off guard, and he thought that life was like the weather – you could never be sure what was coming your way. He was waiting for his father to ring from Cleveland, and he reflected that, if Dad hadn't been detained in the States, the summer would have been very different. He would never have spent time with a working-class family like the Farrellys, or become friends with an Ojibwe girl like Lucy, or jumped off the bridge at Young's Point, or faced down a bully like Moose Packham.

He had really enjoyed his adventures with the G Club, but now he was in two minds about what he wanted most. Part of him wanted to see his father – and wanted to feel that Dad wanted to see *him* – while another part of his brain told him that the sooner Dad arrived in Lakefield, the sooner the fun with Lucy and Mike would end.

His thoughts were interrupted by the ringing of the telephone, and Wilson felt a little surge of excitement as he reached out and lifted the receiver. He was using the phone with the blessing of Dr Mackenzie, the headmaster, but it still felt cheeky to be sitting in a swivel chair behind the school secretary's desk.

'Hello?' he said.

'Wilson? Is that you?'

'Dad!'

'Hello, son. I have some good news for you.'

'You're finished work in Cleveland?'

There was a pause. 'No. No, it's not that. I'm afraid it will take two or three more days to wrap things up. I hope to be with you by Thursday or Friday, though.'

Wilson considered this for a moment. 'Are you driving up in the Bentley?'

'No, I'm not in the mood for motoring. I'll take the train.'

'OK, Dad. So what's the good news, then?'

'I got you the autograph I spoke about. Of Lindbergh, the aviator.'

'Brilliant!' Wilson smiled. Only Dad would describe Lindbergh as 'the aviator' when he was probably the most famous man in the world since flying across the Atlantic. But it was really exciting to have the autograph. 'Wait till I show it to Mike,' he said, 'he'll be dead jealous!'

'Mike?'

'Mike Farrelly. We…we still take sailboats out sometimes.'

Wilson had given a lot of thought to how he would deal with his involvement with the Farrellys. His father had made it clear that he didn't want Wilson socialising intimately with a working-class, Catholic family – but to have made no reference to them at all would sound suspicious after the last conversation they'd had. Wilson hoped that by carefully referring to sailing with Mike he could avoid telling an outright lie, and present it as just two boys enjoying a sport of which his father approved.

'Well…I guess that's all right,' said Dad, 'seeing as there're no other pupils around.'

Mike was relieved at his father's response, though he also found it a bit offensive to suggest that Mike was only OK because there was no-one else.

'And how was Dominion Day?' continued Dad.

'It was good. Dr Mackenzie lead a service in the chapel. And there were fireworks, and a band and fun fair down at the waterfront.' Wilson hoped his father wouldn't ask where he had had dinner.

'So you went into Lakefield?'

'Yes. It would have been very quiet to stay at The Grove.'

'Yes. Yes, I suppose so.'

'And what about you, Dad?' he asked, seeking to deflect attention from himself.

'Dominion Day means nothing in the States, Wilson. So obviously I worked.'

'Right. Sorry…silly question.'

'That's all right. And I'm sorry that we couldn't have been together.'

'Well…we will be, next year,' said Wilson, pleased that his father was being warmer now, and that he hadn't had to lie about dinner with the Farrellys.

'One other thing, Wilson.'

'Yes?'

'This boy…Mike?'

Wilson had no idea what he was going to be asked, and he felt his mouth going dry. 'Yes?'

'I hope you're not at risk by sailing with him.'

'At risk of what, Dad?'

'Being capsized, swept away by currents. Does he know anything about sailing?'

'Yes, he's a good sailor.'

'Really?'

'Yes, why wouldn't he be?'

'He's not a pupil in The Grove, he hasn't been taught like you. People like that don't normally learn sailing.'

Wilson felt a surge of irritation. He resented his father's snobbery in branding the Farrellys as 'people like that'.

'He's actually a better sailor than me, Dad – whatever you think about his people.' It had come out a little sharper than Wilson intended and he hoped he hadn't gone too far. There was a pause, then his father spoke again.

'I don't mean to sound too harsh, Wilson,' he said reasonably. 'It's unfortunate that you've had to stay on in the school, and it's good that this boy has provided companionship.'

'Yes, it would have been pretty miserable on my own,' said Wilson, deciding that he had done enough of trying to make his father feel all right about the situation.

'Point taken,' said Dad. 'As I said before, I'll strongly commend the family to Dr Mackenzie, all right?'

Wilson realised that as a prominent past pupil his father's praise would actually count for something, 'All right, Dad.'

'Fine, we'll leave it at that then. Everything else in order? Cook feeding you up?'

'Yes, everything else is fine.'

'Good. Well, I'm not a great one for the telephone, so we'll talk properly when I see you. Take care, Wilson.'

'You too, Dad.'

'Bye.'

Wilson hung up. He knew his father didn't mean any harm, but he always seemed to feel superior to people who were poorer than him – probably without even realising it. Wilson hoped that he never acted like that in his own dealings with Mike and Lucy. He went back over their friendship in his mind, lost in thought as the rain lashed against the window pane, and eventually decided that he had treated both his new friends as equals, and that his conscience was clear.

Wilson looked up to his father in many ways, but now he made a firm decision. He would never judge people on their class or their religion. He was going to live life differently from his father – whatever the consequences. Buoyed by the decision, he rose from the chair and started back towards his empty dormitory.

Lucy tossed and turned, unable to get to sleep. Outside the wind howled, and the rain pelted against her bedroom window. The log cabin that she shared with her mother was cosy, any gaps in the wood carefully filled with lime, so that normally Lucy enjoyed feeling warm and secure when the elements raged outside. Tonight though she couldn't savour the cosiness of her home – all she could think about was being a witness to murder. Although she hadn't actually seen it happening in the boathouse this afternoon, there was no escaping what she had heard.

Lucy had remained hidden in the shadows after the incident, then had escaped out through the rear of the boathouse when she had heard Mr Packham leaving via the front entrance. Gripped by terror, she hadn't waited to see if a body had been left behind, but instead had fled back along the trail, untied her canoe and paddled away at speed.

She knew that anyone who witnessed a murder was obliged by law to inform the police. But she had been breaking the law herself by trespassing and by being off the reserve without permission. By coming forward she could end up in all sorts of trouble, and perhaps land her mother in trouble as well. They might even say that Mom wasn't a fit guardian, and send Lucy away to a residential school. And then she could forget about the scholarship, and having a career as an artist. There was also the fact that although Lucy had heard the fight, she hadn't actually seen the murder, so could it be said that she was a witness?

She had stayed out on the water for the rest of the afternoon, thinking, then come back to the reserve and had dinner with Mom. Her mother had picked up on her distracted manner and asked if anything was wrong, but Lucy had just claimed to have a bad headache. Mom had given her a herbal drink, and Lucy had gone to bed early.

On the reserve these days, most people were Christians, even though the old traditional beliefs were practiced as well, and Lucy had knelt by her bed and prayed for guidance. She had prayed to Jesus, and she had also asked the Great Spirit of traditional Ojibwe belief to help in her hour of need. But despite the prayers she didn't feel much calmer, and the more she thought about God, the more she wondered if it would be a sin for her to do nothing when a serious crime had been committed. Maybe she should go to the police, she thought, no matter what trouble it brought down upon her.

She wished she could talk it through with someone, but she was afraid to tell Mom. She knew too that her mother tried to avoid contact with the white man's world as much as possible, and she hated the idea of involving her with the police. To say nothing of the trouble she herself would be in with Mom if it all came out about Mike and Wilson, not to mention the trespassing.

She thought of confiding in Anne, but Anne was an awful gossip and couldn't be trusted with a secret this big. Mike and Wilson *could* keep a secret, though. Maybe the boys could help her to decide the best thing to do. Apart from being smart and clued-in about most things, they were also white – which meant they would know more about the workings of the police, and the outside world in general.

The heavy rain lashed against the window, and Lucy hoped the unseasonable bad weather wouldn't last. If it rained tomorrow morning the boys might not show up at the arranged meeting, and now that she had decided to ask their advice she badly wanted to see them.

She turned over and back again in her bed, and added good weather to her other prayers. She wished that this could be just a dream from which she would waken, but of course it wasn't. Still, she would need her energy for whatever decision she reached tomorrow, and so she closed her eyes, turned once more and tried to go to sleep.

CHAPTER TWENTY-FOUR

'**M**y God!' said Mike, 'that's unbelievable!'

'Every word of it is true,' answered Lucy, unhappily.

They were sitting on a tree trunk at their usual meeting place on Webster Island, the air sweet and clear now that last night's storm had blown itself out. The greenery all about them seemed even fresher after the rain, but Mike was oblivious to the beauty of the sunny morning.

'You have to go to the police,' said Wilson, his face revealing his shock at Lucy's tale.

'You really think so?'

'Yes! Look, I know you were trespassing, but that doesn't matter – this is a murder!' He paused. 'Anyway, if you help them catch a murderer you'd be a heroine.'

'Only if they catch him,' cautioned Mike. ' Supposing they don't? Supposing he's already moved the body?'

'Exactly!' said Lucy. 'I want to do what's right, but I don't want to involve my family with the police. *We* could suffer, instead of Packham.'

'But even if he has moved the body,' said Wilson, 'the police could still catch him if you tip them off. They could search his premises, see if he's dug a grave.'

'Or they might find no body, and then claim I was causing trouble.'

Wilson looked confused. 'Why would you want to cause trouble?'

'Moose Packham. He might say I was trying to get at his father, out of spite.'

'I hadn't thought of that. But...I don't think the police are like that.'

Lucy looked Wilson in the eye. 'Have you ever been in trouble with the police?'

'No.'

'Then you don't know what they might be like. If this turns out wrong, I could be in trouble, Mom could be in trouble, I could get sent to one of those awful schools, I could lose my chance of a scholarship.'

Mike could see that his friend was distressed, and he didn't want to add to her worries, but he felt he had to speak up. 'There's something else to weigh up.'

'What?'

'We know now that Packham would murder someone who gets in his way. Maybe that's another reason not to go public.'

Mike could see that Wilson was shocked, but from Lucy's expression he realised that this had already occurred to her.

'I'm not a coward,' she said. 'But I don't want to be his next victim.'

'No, of course not,' said Wilson. 'But there must be something we can do – we can't just let him get away with murder.'

'We're not a hundred percent certain he murdered him,' said Mike.

'I'm ninety-nine percent certain,' said Lucy.

'Right, then,' replied Mike, 'let's take it that he definitely murdered him.' His mind was racing, and now his heart began to thump as he hit on a plan. 'There is something we could do. But it would take a bit of nerve.'

Lucy looked at him sharply. 'What is it?'

'Last night's storm was bad,' said Mike, 'so there's a fair chance he didn't get to move the body. We could make for the boathouse right now, and sneak inside to see if the body is still there. If it is, we call the police straight away.'

'And if it's not?' asked Lucy.

'Then we decide our next move. Who's on to try it?'

Mike watched as his two friends weighed up the suggestion, a part of him half-hoping that they would dismiss it as too risky. Wilson looked uncertain, and Lucy was biting her lip as she tried to come to a decision.

'OK,' she said slowly. 'Let's do it.'

'Sure?'

'Yes.'

Mike turned to Wilson. 'Will?'

The other boy looked like he was holding his breath, then he nodded. 'One for all, all for one. Count me in,' he said.

Despite the seriousness of the situation, Mike found himself smiling in response. 'Right,' he said. 'No time to waste – let's go!'

* * *

Lucy led the way through the woods on the Packham estate. She had warned the two boys not to snap twigs underfoot and to avoid disturbing the foliage, which was still wet and glistening after last night's rain. She managed to move smoothly and at a good pace, but the boys had to concentrate hard to keep up with her without making noise.

They were making for the boathouse from a different direction to Lucy's approach of the previous day. She thought it best to avoid the trail alongside the lake, and instead they had hidden the skiff and canoe at the shoreline, then cut in through the woods with the plan of skirting around to meet the track that led to the rear of the boathouse.

Suddenly Lucy raised her hand and stopped. It was an agreed signal and Wilson and Mike halted immediately. Lucy pointed, and the boys drew nearer to see what she was indicating.

'Tyre marks,' she whispered. They had reached the point where the track cut through the woods. 'Someone drove here this morning.'

'How do you know?' asked Wilson.

'The track is muddy and the tyre marks are clear. But it rained all last night, so the marks must have been made this morning.'

Mike nodded. 'That makes sense.'

'You think maybe Packham moved the body already?' said Wilson.

'Could be.'

'But we still need to check out the boathouse,' said Mike.

'I know,' said Lucy. 'While we do that, one of us should hide here and keep watch on the track. We don't want to be taken by surprise if anyone comes back this way.'

'Good thinking,' said Mike.

'So who wants to come with me to the boathouse?'

'I'll come,' said Wilson.

'Are you sure?' asked Mike.

'Certain.'

'OK,' said Lucy. 'Mike, if anyone approaches from this direction, you come and warn us.'

'Right.'

'But don't leave footprints in the track – run along the grassy verge.'

'OK.'

'Ready, Will?'

'Yeah.'

'Follow in my footsteps,' instructed Lucy, 'it's not too far.'

Mike gave them a thumbs up, then Lucy and Wilson set off again. The track wound through the woods, and within a couple of minutes the boathouse came into sight. There were heavy wooden gates that were closed, and clear tyre marks visible where the muddy track ended at the gates.

'Let me check that there's nobody inside,' whispered Lucy. 'If the coast is clear we'll go in the pedestrian door in the back wall. OK, Will?'

He looked nervous but nodded back. 'OK.'

* * *

Wilson found himself holding his breath as Lucy slipped sound-lessly through the trees, and approached a side window to the boathouse without leaving any footprints. After a moment Lucy turned around and indicated for him to approach. Wilson breathed out, then followed Lucy's route through the wet trees.

'No-one there,' she said.

'Did you see a body?'

'No. We're going to have to go in to check that out.'

Wilson felt butterflies in his stomach but he spoke firmly. 'Let's do it then.'

They crossed to the pedestrian door, and Lucy tried the handle. It was slightly stiff, but it creaked open. Lucy grimaced at the noise, and they both stood stock still. Nothing happened, however, and Lucy stepped inside, with Wilson following close behind.

He was hit by the smell of reedy water and rotting wood, but before he could say anything Lucy made her way forward, then stopped and pointed.

'What?' said Wilson

'This is about where they were standing when I was hiding,' she said.

'So the body has been moved?'

Lucy nodded 'Looks like it. Some of the crates are gone too. He might have put the body into one of them.'

'Let's a have quick look around,' suggested Wilson. 'Just to make sure the body's not shoved away in a corner or an empty crate.'

'OK,' said Lucy. They split up and quickly examined the interior of the boathouse. It was a large, gloomy space but they soon established that there was no corpse to be found.

'I guess it was too much to hope that the body would still be here,' said Lucy.

'Yeah. But hang on a second – look at this,' said Wilson, dropping down on one knee.

'What is it?'

The shady interior didn't have much natural light, but Wilson pointed to a dark stain on the floor. 'I think that might be dried blood,' he said.

Lucy looked uncomfortable. 'That…that makes it real.'

Wilson reached into his pocket and withdrew his penknife.

'What are you doing?'

'Collecting evidence,' he answered. He cut a sliver from the bloodstained wooden floor and slipped it into his handkerchief. 'Might be important if there's a trial.'

'I'd never have thought of that. Smart thinking, Will.'

'Thanks.'

Lucy shivered. 'Come on. Let's get back to Mike.'

They left the boathouse and retraced their trip through the woods. After a few moments Mike stepped forward from where he had been hiding in the shrubbery.

'Well?' he asked eagerly.

'We found dried blood on the floor, but the body is gone,' answered Wilson.

'Blast!' said Mike. 'It would have been good to just call the police.'

'Yeah.'

'It was still worth a try,' said Lucy.

'It was. But I was doing some thinking while you were gone,' said Mike. 'And there's something else we could do.'

Wilson looked at his friend with interest. 'What's that?'

'Why don't we get out of here first?' said Mike. 'Then I'll tell you my plan.'

Lucy guided her canoe towards the heavily wooded shore of Lake Katchewanooka, with the boys following closely behind in the skiff. They moored under the overhanging foliage, out of sight of any passers-by, then climbed out onto the bank.

Lucy turned to Mike, eager to know what he had come up with. 'So, what's your idea?'

'Well, I was thinking – what choices do we actually have?'

'Just two,' answered Wilson. 'We go to the police, or we say nothing. And I can see why you're nervous, Lucy, but I think we should tell.'

Lucy was about to reply but Wilson held up his hand. 'I know the man he killed was another gangster. But he was still a human being.'

Lucy nodded reluctantly. She turned to Mike, hoping he might have some other solution. 'So what's your idea?'

'I think there's a third choice. That we investigate it ourselves.'

'How would we do that?' asked Lucy.

'If Packham has moved the body we could try and find out where it is. Much easier to go to the police if we have hard evidence.'

'Supposing he hasn't just moved it?' said Wilson. 'Supposing he's dumped it in the lake, or buried it on his estate somewhere?'

Mike shook his head. 'I don't think that's likely. If I killed someone I wouldn't dump the corpse near where I live – there's always the chance of a body being discovered. I think Packham would dump it somewhere far away.'

'Like where?' asked Lucy.

'Well, he's a smuggler, right? If it was me, I'd pack the body in a crate with my next lot of illegal booze. Then when it's being shipped to the States the body could end up in a lake or river somewhere. That way, it vanishes hundreds of miles from here.'

Wilson nodded. 'That would make sense.'

Lucy looked at Mike. 'So we'd have to find the body before his next shipment goes out?'

'Yeah.'

'They could hardly go out in the storm last night,' suggested Wilson. 'But for all we know a shipment could be going out today.'

'I doubt if they smuggle liquor in broad daylight,' answered Mike. 'Tonight is probably the earliest it would go. And even then they hardly move stuff over the border every night. That might give us a day or two.'

Lucy considered where that left them. 'So right now he's probably storing the body in a crate, somewhere it wouldn't be noticed.
In his brewery in Peterborough, I guess,' she said.

'That would be my bet,' answered Mike.

'So what do we do?' asked Wilson.

'We make for Peterborough.'

'And then what?' asked Lucy.

Mike shrugged. 'We play it by ear at that stage. But like Will
said, a man has been murdered. It wouldn't be right to just do
nothing.'

Lucy knew that Mike was right and that it would be wrong
to allow Packham to get away with taking another person's life.
But she found the idea of taking him on scary, and going to the
brewery in Peterborough would mean entering his world, where
dangerous, frightening things could happen.

'What do you think, Lucy?' said Mike, his tone gentle. 'In the
end it's up to you.'

Lucy weighed it up, torn between duty and fear. After a moment
she breathed out, then faced the two boys. 'We can't let him away
with it. Let's go to Peterborough.'

CHAPTER TWENTY-FIVE

Ciara strode eagerly across the bridge that spanned the Otonabee River. A fine mist hung in the morning air over where the water cascaded down through the sluices of the navigation channel. She descended a set of steps and entered the riverside park, the early morning sun promising a hot day to come.

She had slept reasonably well, but woken early, her body clock still somewhere between Irish and Canadian time. She had had breakfast with Dad, then explained that she wanted to finish reading Granddad's manuscript, even if it took all morning.

Dad had smiled but understood her eagerness – he was curious himself – and he left her to it, saying that he had some business to attend to in Lakefield. Ciara's original plan had been to read the manuscript in the back garden, but now she was glad that she had acted on a whim and decided to do her reading at the marsh.

She walked along the trail, encountering a lone jogger, but otherwise savouring the sense that she had the place to herself. She reached the marsh and entered its enclosed space, the high reeds swaying in the breeze against a clear blue sky. Looking about her, Ciara reflected on how her grandfather had described visiting this very spot in the manuscript. It gave her a weird feeling to think that her ancestor had acted out dramas right here, and she suddenly felt the hairs rise on the back of her neck.

What would she have done, she wondered, if she had found herself in the situation that Granddad, Lucy and Wilson had faced? She wasn't sure, and she sat down now on a bench and took off her rucksack. Like the members of the G Club had done in the old days, she had brought provisions with her, and she was determined to stay here until she finished the story. Opening the rucksack, she took out the manuscript.

She had grown really fond of the twelve-year-old version of her grandfather, and she also liked the way Wilson had become braver as the story unfolded. But the person she really found herself rooting for was Lucy. Maybe it was because she was a girl too, or maybe it was because Lucy stood to lose much more than the boys if things went wrong. Whatever it was, Ciara wanted things to end well for her, but she was worried.

Looking about, the marsh seemed so serene today, and Lakefield in the early morning appeared sleepy and peaceful – the essence of an attractive Canadian small town. But a murder had happened here, and Ciara wasn't sure that the killing was over. Intrigued by what lay ahead, she sat back on the bench, opened the manuscript and began reading.

CHAPTER TWENTY-SIX

'Are you all right, Mike?'

'Yes. Yes, I'm fine.'

His mother looked at him appraisingly across the kitchen. 'Are you sure? You seem a bit distracted.'

Mike was distracted, and had been thinking about the planned trip to Peterborough. To avoid suspicion Wilson and Mike had kept to their normal routine and returned to The Grove early after lunch. They were to meet Lucy and get the afternoon train from Lakefield station, and Mike's head had been spinning as he tried to figure out how to proceed once they got to the Packham brewery. He cursed himself now, however, for not being more careful in front of Ma. She was smart, and generally in tune to the mood of those around her, and he should have been more aware of that.

'I was just...I was just thinking about Will,' he improvised. 'It's kind of tough not knowing for sure when his father will come to collect him.'

Ma nodded sympathetically. 'Yes, it must be hard. But he seems to be really enjoying his adventures with you.'

If only you knew, thought Mike. 'Yes, we've...we've had fun together,' he answered, trying for a smile.

His mother looked at him again, and Mike wasn't sure if he had convinced her or not.

'Anyway, I'd better head off,' he said, 'I'm going in to the village to meet some of the boys.'

His mother didn't answer at once, and Mike prayed that she wouldn't query him further, or give him some chore that would prevent him going on the mission to Peterborough. 'All right?' he said, trying to keep his tone casual.

'Sure. But Mike?'

'Yes?'

'You'd tell me if anything was bothering you, wouldn't you?'

Part of him wanted to come clean and relieve himself of the burden of his secrets. But if he told Ma any of it she would be worried sick. There seemed no point worrying his mother with Moose's threat to Da's job. He couldn't tell about the terrible incident with Packham either without revealing Lucy's role – which would be a betrayal of her trust. More importantly, if they found proof that Moose's father had murdered somebody, then they would all have much bigger concerns.

If they could find proof. To do that, however, he had to get to Peterborough without arousing any more suspicion with Ma. He hated lying to her but he felt that there was no other choice.

'I'm fine, Ma, really. I know I can always come to you if I need to.' On impulse he reached out and kissed his mother on the cheek. 'See you later.'

He waved in farewell, then walked out of the door before Ma could ask any more questions.

Wilson thought that there were clear advantages to being rich. He was standing at the ticket window of Lakefield train station, and thanks to his generous weekly allowance he didn't need to give a second thought to the cost of buying three train tickets to Peterborough.

He had walked from The Grove to the station with Mike, but Lucy had made her own way. There was no point drawing attention to the fact that the three of them were going about together, and so they had decided to wait until the train had left Lakefield before joining forces.

Lucy was playing along. Although sitting near Mike on one of the station benches, she was reading a comic book, so that to the casual observer it looked like she was travelling alone. There was an element of fun to the deception, and Wilson felt nervous but excited at the idea of being on a secret mission.

He paid for the three return tickets, then stepped out of the wooden building and onto the sunlit platform. He rejoined Mike, ignoring Lucy even though she sat just behind where they were standing. There were several other people waiting for the train, but to his relief none of them was from The Grove.

Just then a horse-drawn buggy drew up at the station entrance. A well-dressed, heavy-set man with grey whiskers and a briefcase stepped down from the buggy and paid the driver. Wilson had never seen him before, and he turned back to Mike, then saw the look of horror on Lucy's face.

'Oh my God!' she whispered. 'It's Mr Staunton!'

Wilson knew that Staunton was the Indian Agent, and that he held power over everyone on Lucy's reserve. If he caught her travelling to Peterborough without permission their plan would be in tatters.

In an instant Lucy was on her feet. 'Distract him so I can hide!' she hissed.

Acting on instinct Wilson stepped forward and blocked Staunton's path. Wilson knew that even his casual clothes were expensive and of high quality – Mike had kidded him the first day about being the best-dressed trespasser ever on Webster Island – and he spoke in his poshest voice, so that the Indian Agent would know that he was dealing with the son of a gentleman.

'Excuse me, sir, could I trouble you for the right time?' Wilson said, hoping he had also blocked Staunton's line of vision onto the station platform. Staunton looked down at Wilson. Asking to be told the time was one of the few claims any child could make on an adult, and by asking in the confident tones of the upper classes he knew that the Indian Agent would find it hard to refuse him.

Staunton sighed, put down a briefcase and drew a fob watch from his waistcoat pocket. 'Five minutes to three.'

'Really?' said Wilson, stalling to give Lucy more time to hide. 'I thought it was earlier.'

'Well, it's not, it's five minutes to three,' answered Staunton.

'Nice watch, sir. Is it Swiss?'

Wilson could tell that Staunton was irritated, but he reckoned that the man's instincts would be to remain courteous when talking to someone wealthy.

Sure enough, the Indian Agent nodded brusquely and answered the question. 'Yes it is, actually. Now if you'll excuse me?'

Wilson couldn't look behind him to check if Lucy had found a hiding place, but he decided to buy her an extra few seconds.

'I'm grateful sir,' he said, as Staunton picked up his briefcase. 'You see I have a watch of my own. Present from my father for my twelfth birthday. But it was losing time, so I've had to leave it with the jeweller to be repaired.'

'Good for you,' said Staunton, and this time he moved forward decisively.

Wilson realised that he couldn't detain him further without his behaviour seeming suspicious and so he slowly stepped aside, hoping that he had bought Lucy enough time.

The Indian Agent walked past, and sat down on the bench where Lucy had been reading. Wilson looked about but there was no sign of Mike or Lucy. He felt a surge of relief. Then he heard the sound of an approaching train. In three or four minutes they would somehow have to board a carriage without being seen by Staunton. But first he had to find his friends, and give them their tickets. He turned around and made for the rear of the station.

* * *

The train whistle gave a loud shriek, and the engine rounded a bend as the track followed the curve of the Otonabee River. The surface of the water glistened in the afternoon sunshine, and Lucy looked out the window as the landscape rolled past. She had travelled by train with her mother several times, but she still found it magical to glide through the countryside with a different vista unfolding with each passing moment.

She had hidden in the waiting room while Wilson had distracted Mr Staunton, then Mike had watched to see which carriage the Indian Agent would board. Staunton had entered the first carriage, and so the three friends had slipped into the rear of the second carriage.

They had agreed that they would give Staunton plenty of time to disembark at Peterborough before getting off themselves, and now Lucy felt more relaxed. Their carriage was mostly empty, but if anyone asked them the purpose of their journey they had an answer ready. Peterborough had a lock on the Trent Severn waterway that was the highest hydraulic lift lock in the world, and they would claim that they were going to there, so that Lucy could sketch the lock with her charcoals.

As the boys chatted, Lucy gazed out the window, admiring the broad sweep of the Otonabee. Then her attention was caught by a comment Wilson made to Mike about something called the Orange Order, and she looked at him with curiosity.

'What's that?' she asked.

'Have you really never heard of the Orange Order?' said

Wilson, the surprise evident in his voice. 'It's got members all over Ontario.'

'Not on our reserve,' said Lucy.

'Well, no, I suppose not.'

'So what is it?'

'It's…it's like a club for people who support Canada's link with Britain. People who are for the Crown.'

'Right,' said Lucy. 'And what do you have to do to join?'

'Eh… you have to be Protestant, and be in favour of the Queen and the Union and all that.'

'And what do they do?'

'They have marches, and gatherings, and…generally they look after each other.'

'How do they look after each other?'

Wilson shrugged. 'Getting each other jobs and things like that.'

'Can girls join?'

'No, it's only for men.'

'So if you're not a man, and you're not a Protestant, they won't give you a job?'

Wilson looked slightly taken aback. 'Well…I…I don't think it's exactly like that.'

'No?' said Mike.

Lucy looked Wilson in the eye. 'What you really mean is that you've never looked at it that way before.'

Wilson smiled sheepishly. 'Well…no. Maybe I didn't see it from that point of view.'

Lucy liked him for his openness. 'At least you're honest,' she said. 'But why won't they let girls in?'

'I don't know,' admitted Wilson. After a moment he looked at her with a hint of challenge. 'Do girls get to do everything in your tribe?'

Lucy hesitated. She knew that even though her own mother had status on the reserve as a herbalist and healer, most of the power in the tribe lay with the men. 'No,' she answered. 'They don't.'

'There you are then,' said Wilson.

'But they *should* be able to do everything.'

'Well, there's loads of things that *should* be, Lucy,' said Mike sympathetically, 'but that's how things are.'

'Things can change though. Who'd have believed twenty years ago that someone like Lindbergh could fly across the Atlantic?'

'Fair point,' said Mike.

Lucy felt the train slowing, and she looked out of the window again. They were starting the approach to Peterborough, and up ahead she could see a railway bridge that spanned the river. The train station was on the far bank and soon they would reach their stop. She would have liked to continue the discussion but there were more urgent things to be done, and so she put everything else from her mind and prepared for what lay ahead.

CHAPTER TWENTY-SEVEN

Mike walked confidently in through the gates of Maple Brewery. It was in an industrial area several blocks southwest of the train station, but Wilson had borrowed a map of Peterborough from the school library and the three friends had found the brewery without difficulty.

Wilson had been dispatched to walk the circumference of the brewery site and to check for other entrances or exits. Lucy was across the road, apparently doing a charcoal sketch of the premises, but actually keeping a lookout while Mike did his reconnaissance inside the brewery.

Mike carried a large manila envelope and walked purposefully as though he knew where he was going. Lots of large companies employed boy messengers who delivered post and ran errands, and he hoped that if he behaved as though he had a right to be here, then he could avoid being challenged.

He made his way along what looked like the main brewery yard, encouraged by the fact that he wasn't drawing attention from any of the men working there. There were labourers loading grain from a cart into long metal containers on wheels, and maintenance men carrying out repairs to a large wooden vat that lay on its side on the ground. There was a pungent brewing smell in the air, but Mike made certain not to screw up his nose. No point letting anyone see that he was new to this environment, he thought.

His plan was to try to find the part of the brewery from which shipments were despatched, and he was trying to decide which way to go. He heard the sound of a lorry and he glanced around to see that a vehicle had come in through the main gate. The lorry contained empty barrels and Mike stood aside to let it pass, then followed in its wake.

The lorry was travelling slowly and Mike was able to follow it without having to increase his pace. He saw a sign that said No. 2 Vathouse and Traffic Department, with an arrow indicating left. The lorry turned left, and Mike did likewise.

After a moment the lorry stopped. The driver's assistant got out of the cab, then gave hand signals to the driver as the lorry was reversed into a loading bay. Mike skirted the vehicle and strode on into a large warehouse with more loading bays and hundreds of wooden casks stored along the length of the building.

He reasoned that the Traffic Department would organise the despatch of liquor and the return of empty containers. If his theory was right, and the body of the murdered man was likely to be dumped on an illegal liquor run to the US border, then the consignment might well pass through here. Then again, maybe this was where perfectly legal activity took place, and the illicit shipments might be stored elsewhere, and shifted under cover of darkness.

Either way, Mike knew that this was where his mission became dangerous. He had to find evidence to bring to the police, but the deeper he went into the brewery, the greater was the chance of him being caught snooping. His pulse was racing and part of him wanted to run away back to safety. But he paused a moment, steeling himself, then continued on his way.

He kept his eyes peeled for the type of crates that Lucy had described as being in the boathouse, but most of the space here was taken up with rows of wooden barrels. He noted the names that had been chalked onto boards above each section he passed: Millbrook, Campbelltown, Norwood. The city of Windsor was a major smuggling point for running liquor across the Detroit River into the US state of Michigan, so he was on the lookout for the name Windsor, or possibly Buffalo, which was a nearer American destination in the state of New York.

He came to a junction and noted that to the right were rows of long crates instead of barrels. These could contain whiskey or rum, and looked more promising. He turned right, then started checking the names of the nearest consignments. All of them were for local destinations, but there were many more crates stretching into the distance.

Mike was about to move on when a guttural voice stopped him dead.

'Help you, sonny?'

Mike turned around, trying not to let his fear show.

The man was in overalls, and Mike suspected that he was a worker rather than a supervisor. Mike still held the manila envelope as a prop. But that had been intended to make it look from a distance as though he were a messenger. If he tried to play that role now the man might ask what the message was, and who it was for. Instead Mike opted for his other cover story, and tried for an innocent smile.

'I hope you can help me, sir. I'm doing a project for my school – is it true that you can do a tour of the brewery here?'

'Are you kidding me?'

'No, sir. Some companies do tours, and–'

The man interrupted him with a humourless laugh. 'Not this company.'

'Too bad. Thanks anyway, sir,' said Mike, starting to move off.

'Hang on a second. How did you end up in here?'

'I walked up the yard – I was following a lorry full of barrels. And then I looked into the traffic department and it seemed fascinating. I'm really interested in industry, that's why I'm doing the school project.' Mike indicated the manila folder.

The man said nothing but looked back impassively. Mike prayed that he would believe the story, and he hoped his anxiety wasn't showing.

Finally the man spoke. 'Next time you're doing a project, get permission before you start trespassing. Got that?'

'Yes, sir, I will,' said Mike. He gave the man a quick nod, then turned and walked away, his heart pounding.

✶ ✶ ✶

The dipping sun shone in through the stained-glass windows, bathing the church in soft coloured light. A worried Wilson knelt in the school chapel with his head bowed. He wasn't overly religious but tonight he needed all the support and guidance he could get. From where he knelt Wilson could see the memorial window that commemorated the past pupils who had died in the Great War. He tried to draw inspiration from their willingness to give their lives for what they believed in, and he told himself that he too should follow in the school tradition, and do what was right, whatever the risk.

Of course the deceased past pupils had been fighting for king and country, whereas Wilson's task of bringing a gangster to justice seemed less noble. Even so, murder was a foul crime, and Wilson knew he couldn't live with himself if he didn't support Lucy and Mike in seeking evidence against Brent Packham. There was also the fact that Packham was Moose's father – and he had had enough of bullies. No, he thought, whatever happened, he had to go ahead.

This afternoon's visit to the brewery had yielded valuable intelligence about the layout of the site, and later tonight they were planning a return visit. Under cover of darkness they were going to gain entry when there would be few staff about, the plan being to have a thorough examination of the storage areas in the hope of finding the body.

One part of Wilson wondered if they were clutching at straws. There was no guarantee that Packham hadn't already disposed of the corpse somewhere in the Lakefield area. And even assuming that he hadn't, they couldn't be sure that he would have taken it to the brewery. He could have ordered some of his henchmen to dispose of the body somewhere else entirely. On the other hand what better way to move a body off his estate than in the wooden crates that Lucy had seen at the boathouse? And if he was moving illicit liquor at night, there would certainly be a logic to dumping the body during the next illegal run.

He wished that time could be wound back, and that Lucy had gone to the police immediately after the incident in the boat-house. Then they could have carried on as normal with the G Club and not become embroiled with a dangerous gangster like Packham. But he understood Lucy's reasons, and there were good grounds now for not going to the police until they had solid evidence.

He tried to still the voice in his head that said his father would be horrified with what he was doing. But Dad wasn't here, which surely meant that Wilson was entitled to make his own decision. So be it, he thought now, he would back his friends, for better or worse. He lifted his head and looked up at the altar. He prayed one last time for the strength to be brave, than he rose from the kneeler and made for the door of the chapel, eager for darkness to fall and to be on his way.

Lucy desperately wanted to go to bed. Her mother, however, was in no rush to turn in for the night, as they sat in the kitchen sipping mugs of cocoa by the soft glow of an oil lamp. Lucy's plan was to meet up with Mike and Wilson at the train station and to take the final evening train back to Peterborough. The train left at 11.30pm, which meant that Lucy had to appear to go to bed and then slip out unnoticed.

'I think your art is really coming on,' said her mother now. 'Your watercolours are wonderful.'

'Thanks, Mom.'

'If there's any justice you'll get that scholarship.'

'I sure hope so.'

Her mother looked slightly wistful. 'I always thought you'd follow me as a healer. I mean, already you know a lot about herbs. But now…I think I need a new apprentice.'

'Yeah?'

'That won't be your job. I think you could be a great artist, Lucy. Maybe the first Ojibwe artist to be famous across Canada.'

Lucy smiled. 'Thanks, Mom. But let's try and get the scholarship first, and then conquer Canada!'

Her mother smiled in return, then spoke seriously. 'All right. But never doubt what you can achieve, Lucy. Other people will try to hold you back, it's important you don't let them, that you follow your course.'

'Thanks, Mom. And…and thanks for everything – you've been great.' Lucy's eyes slid to the clock on the mantel. It was 10.30pm.

She was touched by her mother's faith in her, and she thought once more how lucky she was. She knew that Mom would miss her if she moved to the city to study art, and she loved her for being so generous in spirit as to still encourage her. She felt guilty about wanting to end the conversation, but she couldn't let her friends down by missing the train, and time was moving on.

She felt bad too about deceiving Mom, but she consoled herself that her mother believed that life was sacred. Mom wouldn't want Brent Packham to get away with killing someone, and although Lucy was going behind her back, she was doing it for the right reasons. But that would only be possible if she got to bed soon.

She yawned and stretched out her arms.

'Tired?' said Mom.

'Yeah, I'm pretty bushed. I think I'll turn in. How about you?'

Lucy had kept the question casual sounding, but she really hoped that Mom wasn't planning to stay up late.

Her mother shrugged. 'Yes, I think I'll turn in too.'

Lucy felt relieved and she stood up. She reached over and kissed her mother on the cheek.

''Night, Mom.'

''Night, Lucy.'

Lucy took both their mugs and carried them to the kitchen sink. Then she made for the bedroom, hoping that she could still carry out her plan, and make it to the train station on time.

CHAPTER TWENTY-EIGHT

Ciara was transfixed, oblivious to the summer sounds of droning insects and the soft whistle of the breeze through the reeds. She had been horrified to read of the man being beaten to death in the boathouse, yet fascinated by the daring of Granddad and his friends in trying to bring Brent Packham to justice. It was hard to believe that murder had been committed right here in peaceful Lakefield, and even more strange to think that her lovable grandfather had been in the thick of the drama.

Ciara was at the point in the story where Granddad and his friends were planning their night raid on Maple Brewery and she was seriously worried on their behalf. She found herself praying that they would come out of it safely, then she realised that what she was doing made no sense. Whatever had happened had already taken place almost ninety years ago – and all the praying in the world couldn't change the past.

In most of the mystery novels that Ciara had read she identified with the leading character, but it had never occurred to her that she would encounter a murder mystery in real life. And due to her link with Granddad she almost felt a part of the story, and she wondered what she would have done if she had been a member of his gang back in 1928.

She hoped that she would have been as brave as the others in the G Club, but she wasn't sure if she would have had the nerve to fool her parents the way they had. Of course it was different all those years ago, when there were no mobile phones or texting. Parents then weren't so involved with their children's activities, and kids had more freedom.

One thing hadn't changed, however, and Ciara knew that she had inherited her grandfather's dislike of bullies. She had found herself really disliking Moose Packham and his thuggish father, and she hoped that they would get their just deserts. But she also knew that real life often didn't work out according to plan, and so she wasn't sure if they would.

The morning sun had grown hotter, and Ciara drank from her water bottle, but her picnic lay untouched. She told herself that she would take a break for a snack in another half hour. Meanwhile she couldn't wait to find out what happened next, and she eagerly turned the next page of the manuscript and read on.

CHAPTER TWENTY-NINE

Mike cursed the full moon. Normally he loved the way moonlight gave a landscape an ivory glow, but tonight he would have preferred the cover of darkness.

'Don't stare at the moon, Mike!' whispered Lucy, 'it affects your night vision.'

'Right,' he said, turning away at once.

They had got to Peterborough without incident. Now they were at the rear of Maple Brewery, at an area that Wilson had identified during his reconnaissance earlier in the day. It was just after midnight and all the entrance gates to the brewery were closed, as they had expected. Wilson, however, had found a point at the rear of the brewery where the boundary wall dipped a little. The plan was to scale the wall and make their way into the grounds. Once inside they would head for the loading areas that Mike had found. Wilson had borrowed three flash lamps from the school – with just a skeleton staff on duty in The Grove he had a lot of freedom – and they intended to use the flash lamps to search every nook and cranny in the traffic department.

The vast majority of the brewery staff would not be on duty this late at night, yet there were still some lights showing.

'I reckon that could mean an illegal liquor run is on for tonight,' said Mike. 'We need to act before the crates get shipped out.'

He felt a tap on his shoulder.

'See that big cloud?' said Wilson. 'Soon it will block the moon.'

Mike nodded. 'We'll move as soon as it does.'

Earlier they had found some discarded wooden boxes, and the plan was to place the boxes against the wall, climb up onto them and then cross the brewery wall. If they found nothing in the brewery, they would make their way back to Lakefield and be in bed before anyone knew that they had ever gone. But far better would be to return in glory with a police escort – if they found the body and Packham was arrested for murder. Mike realised that they might be in trouble with their parents at first, but they would also be heroes who had prevented a killer from escaping justice, and that would justify all they had done.

Still, one step at a time, he thought as he looked up once more at the night sky. The cloud started to cross the face of the moon.

'OK. Let's move,' said Mike.

Wilson switched off his flash lamp and inched forward in the gloom of the warehouse. The three friends had quickly made their way through the brewery site, with Mike picking out the route to the traffic department. Once there, they entered through the loading bays, then separated, each of them to search a different area of the large rambling despatch and storage areas.

Now Wilson drew nearer to a lighted office that was at the end of an aisle of wooden casks. He felt his stomach tightening with fear. There was a man standing in the office and he was speaking on the telephone. The man was tall and well built. He had dark hair, a sallow complexion, and was smartly dressed. Brent Packham, thought Wilson, as he tried to calm his rapid breathing. His instincts were to turn and run, but he couldn't abandon his friends. Instead he forced himself to advance so that he could listen in on the conversation.

Wilson could feel sweat forming on his forehead and he paused to wipe it away with his handkerchief, then silently drew nearer to the office door, keeping carefully to the shadows. He could see now that the office had sinks and glass jars of liquid along one wall, and he realised that it also acted as a small laboratory. Packham had his back to the door, and Wilson crept closer. He was confident that in looking out from the lighted office into the darkened storage area Packham wouldn't be able to see him. He strained his ears to listen.

'I don't care if his wife is sick,' Packham said into the phone. 'I don't care if his wife is dying! Just tell him to be there when the lorries arrive!'

Was that about a shipment going out? thought Wilson.

'It has to be tonight,' insisted Packham. 'Everything is set at the border.'

The other person must have accepted Packham's order, because now he sounded more at ease. 'Yeah, the guys should be getting here in about half an hour.'

Wilson swallowed hard. They had less than thirty minutes to

find the body – if the body was even here. He needed to act.

Packham had finished his conversation and hung up, and Wilson began backing away into the darkened warehouse. Suddenly his foot hit against something metallic, making a noise. The sound hadn't been particularly loud but Packham immediately looked out into the darkness, his face watchful.

Wilson froze. He told himself that there was no reason for the man to assume that the sound had been an intruder. Breweries stored grain, and he had read about cats being kept to keep the mice down. Maybe Packham would write it off as the movement of a late night animal.

Packham made for the office door, but the man didn't look alarmed. All the same Wilson backed further down the darkened side aisle. He flattened himself up against a row of wooden casks and held his breath as he saw Packham passing the entrance to the aisle.

Packham's footsteps faded away, and Wilson breathed out. He waited for a moment, giving Packham plenty of time to go wherever he was going. But now that Packham was on the loose their mission was more dangerous. Maybe they should quit while they were ahead and just get out of the brewery. But there was half an hour before Packham's men arrived, enough time to find what they came for – if they were lucky. He stood there for another moment trying to decide what to do.

Wilson felt a sharp jab to his shoulder. He spun around in shock, and found to his horror that he was face to face with Brent Packham.

Before Wilson could say a word the man sent him sprawling with a smack to the face. Wilson fell back against the casks, then immediately was dragged to his feet again. Packham jerked him forward. Their faces were only inches apart, and Wilson could smell mint on the man's breath. Packham tightened his grip, then spoke venomously. 'Just what the hell are you doing?!'

Lucy stopped dead. The beam from her flash lamp quivered, but she stilled her shaking hand. She had found destination names chalked onto blackboards in each of the sections of the traffic department that she had checked. All the names so far had been of local Canadian towns, but this one read Buffalo, which was across the border in the USA. This could be it – an illegal consignment of liquor that was to be smuggled into America. And unlike the shipments that were made up of casks of beer, this one had the kind of large wooden crates that she had seen in the boathouse. She lowered the beam of the flash lamp and scanned the shipment. It was a large consignment and it took time to check out each box. Her beam came to rest on a crate that was tucked in behind most of the others. Lucy saw water on the floor beneath the crate, and her heart rate quickened.

Despite last night's storm, the weather had mostly been hot since yesterday's killing in the boathouse. Mike had said the body might be packed in ice, and now there was water on the floor around this crate, but not any others.

Lucy stood unmoving for a moment, then she made herself go closer. She approached the crate and dropped to her hunkers, playing the beam over the wooden surface. It was certainly large enough to hold a body, especially if the corpse was doubled up. Lucy paused. She had seen dead people before. But there was a world of difference between seeing Ojibwe dead being honoured in a traditional ceremony and in seeing the body of a man who had been brutally murdered.

Yet the whole point of coming here was to see that justice was done. And that meant finding out if the dead body was actually hidden in the crate. Lucy took a deep breath, then reached out to open the lid.

The lid wouldn't budge. It didn't seem to be nailed shut, but even when she used all her strength she couldn't get the lid to open. There was only one thing for it. She would have to go back and get one of the others to help. Rising from her hunkers, she shone the beam carefully to light her way, then went to find her friends.

Mike saw a light in the distance and switched off his flash lamp. Since he had split up with Wilson and Lucy he had ventured deep into the depths of the gloomy warehouse. The place wasn't in total darkness, due to infrequently placed overhead lamps that provided pools of light, but he couldn't make out the figure behind the flash lamp. He backed up against the wall, straining his eyes to see who it was that was approaching. After a moment he realised that it was

Lucy. He breathed out in relief, switched his own light back on and called out in a whisper, 'Lucy! Over here!'

He saw her start, then she approached swiftly.

'Mike, I think I might have found it! There's a shipment for Buffalo. And one of the boxes is leaking, like you might get from melting ice.'

Mike felt the hairs go up on the back of his neck. 'Really?'

'Yeah. I tried to open the box, but it's too stiff – I need help.'

'Where is it?'

'Follow me.'

Lucy turned and started back, and Mike followed on her heels, hopeful but scared at the thought of what they might find.

Wilson struggled with all his might, but the water forced its way up his nostrils and down his throat. He was drowning. All of a sudden he was yanked upwards by his hair. He coughed and spluttered as he gasped in lungfuls of oxygen. Brent Packham had been dunking Wilson's head into a sink full of water in the laboratory part of the office, and now he spoke with quiet menace.

'Next time you drown! One last chance, kid. Tell me why you're here.'

Wilson's mind was racing. He had tried lying to Packham, claiming that he had broken into the brewery to see if there was anything to steal. It had been the first thing that came into his head, but Packham had scoffed, citing Wilson's accent and high-quality clothing as unlikely features in a petty thief.

'OK, kid, don't talk then,' said Packham now. 'See how you like drowning!' He forced Wilson's head towards the sink.

'All right! All right!' cried Wilson.

'Talk!'

'I broke in…I broke in to find evidence.'

'Of what?'

'That you…that you…'

'That I *what*?'

'That you killed a man.'

Packham's eyes narrowed. 'What are you talking about?'

Wilson hesitated, and Packham shook him violently.

'I asked you a question!'

'In the boathouse,' said Wilson. 'My friend was hiding there and saw you kill a man. We… we thought you might be keeping the body here.'

'You snooping brat!' cried Packham and he smacked Wilson in the face again.

Wilson reeled from the blow, but before he could react Packham grabbed him by the lapels and pulled him close.

'Who's this friend of yours?'

'It doesn't matter. I was the one who decided to come here. I came alone.' Wilson was desperately trying to come up with a story that wouldn't implicate Mike and Lucy.

'*Who's the friend?*'

'I told you it doesn't—'

Before Wilson could finish the sentence Packham grabbed him by the hair. Wilson opened his mouth to object, and then he was gagging and swallowing water as his head was forced once more into the sink.

'On a count of three,' said Mike, 'OK?'

'OK.'

He was crouched with Lucy at the crate, and they had both worked their fingers under the rim of the wooden lid.

Mike's hands were slippery with perspiration. He took a deep breath then nodded to Lucy. 'One, two, three!'

They both pressed upwards with all of their strength, and Mike felt a creak, but the lid remained in place.

'Again,' he said. 'One, two, *three!*'

With a massive effort, they snapped the lid free. Mike prayed that the sound wouldn't be heard elsewhere, then his mind was diverted by the sight before him. The inside of the crate was lined with a fine-woven sack that was filled with ice, some of which had now melted and leaked out onto the floor

'Mike…' said Lucy, pointing at the contents of the crate.

Underneath the ice, a shape was evident. Steeling himself, Mike reached both hands into the icy water and pushed aside the loosely packed lumps of ice.

'Oh my God!' Lucy gasped. Mike drew back himself, shocked.

Clearly visible under the ice was the face of a man. A dead man.

'Is that…is that him?' asked Mike.

Lucy nodded wordlessly, then found her voice. 'Yes,' she answered shakily. 'Yes, that's him.'

Wilson squirmed and kicked and struggled, but Packham held his head down in the laboratory sink with a vice-like grip. Wilson's chest was pounding, and his lungs felt like they were going to explode. He had thought the gangster was just trying to terrify him. Now he feared that the man really was going to drown him. Even as he fought for his life, he felt sadness at the thought of never again seeing his family or friends.

Then suddenly Packham yanked his head out of the water.

Once more, Wilson coughed and spluttered, as he gulped down mouthfuls of air.

'Think that was your end, kid?' asked Packham.

Wilson didn't answer, instead gasping oxygen into his burning lungs.

'I said, *did you think that was your end?*'

'Yes!'

'Now you know what it's like. And next time it *will* be the end. So I'm going to ask you once more. It's not that big a deal giving a name. Do you really want to lose your life instead?'

It was a horrible choice, and Wilson tried to grapple with it.

'Fine,' said Packham. 'Be a martyr!'

'No! No!' screamed Wilson as the man grabbed him by the head again. 'Her name…her name is Lucy.'

'Lucy what?'

'Lucy Neadeau.'

'Where does she live?'

'Otonabee Reserve.'

'A snooping Redskin!' said Packham angrily. 'Did she come with you tonight?'

'No,' answered Wilson at once.

'Liar!' said Packham. He grabbed Wilson and dragged him across the room. He pushed him into a swivel chair beside the desk, then pulled open a drawer and took out a roll of cord. Packham roughly tied his hands to the chair. Wilson cried out in pain as the cord cut into his wrists, but Packham ignored him and quickly tied his feet to the chair also. When Wilson was totally immobile Packham took a pistol from a shoulder holster inside his jacket.

'Time to find Miss Lucy Neadeau,' he said, with a nasty grin.

Wilson reacted on pure instinct. Screaming at the top of his voice, he roared, 'Run, Lucy! Run Mike! Run for your lives!'

Packham swung around and smacked Wilson in the face. The chair went spinning backward and the last thing that Wilson saw was Packham running out of the door, the gun in his hand and murder in his eyes.

* * *

Lucy swallowed hard. The scream was in the distance, but there was no mistaking Wilson's voice. Her friend had been captured. Even as she felt a stab of fear, she admired his bravery in trying to warn them.

They had been lowering the lid back onto the crate, so as not to alert any of Packham's men while they went for the police. None of that mattered now. Lucy threw the lid down, then rose swiftly from her hunkers, Mike did the same and they started to run back the way they had come.

Lucy heard running steps somewhere behind them, and a man's voice roared out: 'Stop! Stop, or I'll shoot!'

'Don't stop!' panted Lucy to Mike. She reckoned that the man, whoever it was, might be bluffing. But the hunter in Lucy knew that if he did have a gun, it would require exceptional marksmanship to hit a moving target, at distance, in a darkened warehouse. Sure enough, no shot rang out, but her heart was thumping in her chest when she reached a tee junction just a shade behind Mike.

'Split up!' he cried. 'Split up and get the police!'

Mike veered left, and without slowing, Lucy veered right.

There seemed to be only one pursuer, and Mike's tactic was smart. Lucy sprinted on into the darkened depot, turning left and right at random between rows of wooden barrels. After a moment, she realised that she could no longer hear the running steps of the pursuer. The man must have followed Mike. Lucy looked behind. There was neither sight nor sound of anyone.

She ducked in behind a row of casks and tried to get her breath back. Part of her was relieved that the man hadn't followed her, but immediately she felt guilty at the thought, knowing he must be chasing Make. Get to the police, Mike had said, but Lucy had completely lost her bearings by now. Which way led out of the brewery, and which way might bring her back into danger? She didn't know. She paused fearfully, trying to decide what to do next.

Mike sprinted through the darkened warehouse, zigzagging for fear of being shot. He knew better than to waste precious time by looking behind him and instead he ran flat out. He could tell from the sounds of pursuit that he, rather than Lucy, was the one being followed and he tried not to give way to panic.

He raced deeper into the brewery complex, then reached a door at the end of an aisle. Without pausing, Mike pulled the door open and ran through, swinging it shut behind him. Gleaming rows of huge, steel tanks stretched out ahead of him. A sign on the wall read 'Number One Vathouse'.

His nostrils were hit by a yeasty smell, and high above him were catwalks, approached by metal stairways that allowed access to the tops of the vats. Without breaking stride Mike swiftly ascended one of the stairways, taking the steps two at a time. He hoped that his pursuer would expect him to keep running and that by hiding aloft he might shake him off.

Mike climbed as quickly as he could. He reached the highest level of the catwalks almost thirty feet above ground level. The door that Mike had swung shut now burst open, and the man pursuing him ran into view. The vathouse was lit better than the warehouse had been, and Mike prayed that he hadn't been seen rounding the upper circumference of the vat. He stayed stock still now, his breathing ragged, desperately hoping that the man would run on through the vathouse.

To his dismay, Mike realised instead that the footsteps had ceased. Was the man looking around? Or had he glimpsed Mike as he tried to run out of sight high above the vathouse floor?

A moment later he heard a sound that made his stomach plummet. The man was ascending the same stairway Mike had, and coming onto the catwalks.

Mike could see a door in the wall at the end of the row of vats and he rose from where he had been crouching. No point hiding now, when the man would undoubtedly flush him out. Instead he shot out into view, making for the door that he hoped might lead outside. Mike grabbed for the handle.

'Stop!' cried the man from the stairway.

Mike frantically pushed at the door. It didn't budge. He rattled the handle and barged against the door with his shoulder. It still didn't move. He was trapped.

The man's voice rang out again, this time much nearer.

'Hands on your head! Hands on your head, or I shoot!'

Mike saw the man approaching. He had a lethal-looking pistol held in a double-handed grip, and it was aimed unwaveringly at Mike's chest. Now they were close enough for Mike to recognise the man from the Dominion Day celebrations. It was Brent Packham.

Mike felt a chill at being at the mercy of a gangster, and raised his hands high in the air.

'Down on your knees!' he barked. 'On your knees, *now!*'

Mike knelt. He flinched as Packham placed the gun against his temple.

'Who else knows about the boathouse?' he asked.

'No-one!'

'You kids must have told someone!' said Packham pressing the gun hard against Mike's skin. 'Who else did you tell?'

'No-one, I swear!' answered Mike. 'We had no proof – that's why we came to look here!'

Mike could hardly breathe for fear and his knees were trembling. If Packham didn't believe him he might well be shot.

'You better not be lying!'

Mike felt a moment of relief as the gun was removed from his temple. But it was all too temporary. Because even if Packham believed him, he could bury the story for good by making sure that he, Wilson and Lucy didn't get out of the brewery. Mike had given the information to stop Packham from shooting him. But now that the gangster knew the situation, it made sense for him to shoot all three of them. Mike felt a wave of fear and he lowered his head in despair.

Wilson strained his right wrist against the cord. Although his ankles were tied to the swivel chair he had been able to place his feet on the ground and propel the chair towards the desk in Packham's office. Now his fingertips were scrabbling for the handle of a ceramic mug that sat on the desk. The cord bit painfully into Wilson's flesh, but he concentrated on trying to grip the mug. His fingertips brushed frustratingly against the rim but he couldn't quite grasp it.

He forced himself not to panic, then he tried moving the swivel chair with his feet, seeking to inch his hand nearer the mug. Once more he stretched painfully against his bonds, and this time he was rewarded by his index finger slipping inside the handle of the mug. Moving his finger very carefully, he drew the mug towards him until it was near enough for him to grasp the handle.

He placed his feet on the floor again and cast off, propelling the chair backwards. When he was several feet back, Wilson shuffled in the chair to point it at the stone wall to the side of the desk. Once again he placed his feet on the ground, but this time he propelled the swivel chair forward as fast as he could, holding the mug out firmly in front of him. The swivel chair crashed into the stone wall, and the mug smashed.

Wilson kept a firm grip on the handle, which was now attached to a jagged piece of the broken mug. Twisting the handle in his fingers, he placed the jagged edge against the cord that bound him. Because of the angle at which his wrists were tied, he found it hard to get much leverage, but he was able to move the cutting edge of the mug across a small part of the cord. Every movement made the cord bite into his flesh but, ignoring the pain, he sawed as hard as he could against his bonds.

Lucy crept from behind a barrel and looked out across the warehouse. She had no idea which way led deeper into the brewery and which way led out. She had followed Mike's lead earlier, rather than navigating herself, and she cursed herself for not being more aware of her surroundings.

In the confusion of fleeing her pursuer she had changed direction at random. But if she were to have a chance of alerting the police she had to pick a direction and risk exposing herself to capture. She started to move out into the aisle, when suddenly she heard the distant shout of a man's voice.

'It's all over, Lucy!' the voice cried. 'The doors are locked and I have your friends! There's no escape!'

Lucy immediately recognised the voice from the day in the boathouse, but the words shocked her. Could it be true? Could he really have sealed off her escape route so quickly? Or was he lying to trick her?

'If you don't come in, I'm going to shoot Mike. But first I'm going to make him suffer. Have a listen.'

Mike screamed in pain, and Lucy felt sick.

'You can stop it, Lucy. Follow the sound of my voice and give yourself up. You can't escape anyway, so save me the bother of hunting you down!'

Lucy hated the idea of letting Mike suffer, but if she surrendered what was to stop Packham shooting her too? On the other hand Wilson had originally shouted the warning, and maybe he had escaped. If she handed herself in, it could use up a lot of time – time in which Wilson might get to the police.

She stood, unmoving, trying to decide what to do.

Mike was in agony. In order to make him scream, Packham had pinned him to the catwalk and twisted his arm so far up his back that Mike had thought it would snap. Even though he had eased his grip now, Mike's muscles ached, and he despised Packham even more than his son. Mike remembered how Moose had twisted Wilson's arm halfway up his back on the day of the fight in the dormitory, but it was worse when a grown man bullied a boy. Even more awful, however, was the knowledge that this bully had a gun, and that he had good reason to silence Mike and his friends permanently.

The thought of dying was scarier than anything he had ever faced before, but he tried not to give up hope. His best chance of survival was if Wilson got away and raised the alarm. But if Lucy surrendered now, then Packham might kill them both before Wilson got back with the police. He had to stop Lucy from doing that.

He dreaded to think what Packham might do to him if he tried to warn her off. But he would rather go down fighting than passively allow his captor a free hand. His mouth was dry with fear and his limbs were trembling, but he knew he had to gather his nerve. He swallowed hard to get moisture into his throat, then filled his lungs with air. Do it! he told himself, do it now!

'Don't surrender, Lucy!' he roared, 'Whatever you do, *don't surrender!*'

Mike felt a jolt of agonising pain as Packham viciously twisted his arm and slammed him against the metal handrail of the catwalk. But his warning had been loud and clear and, despite his pain, he felt a sense of triumph.

Wilson sawed the broken mug against the last strand of the cord that bound his wrist. The cord finally snapped, and Wilson dropped the mug to the floor. He felt the blood flowing back into his freed limb. He reached across his body and untied his other wrist, then bent down and undid the bonds on his ankles.

His limbs throbbed from where the cord had bitten into his flesh, but he ignored the pain and rose swiftly from the chair.

He had heard Packham shouting to Lucy and knew that Mike was captured and being mistreated. It made him furious and, although he was still frightened, he had decided that it was time to stop running scared from Packham. And by escaping he would have the element of surprise on his side. Time to take the battle to the enemy, he thought.

But he needed a weapon. He looked around the room, seeking a way to arm himself.

✱ ✱ ✱

Lucy heard a shot and she stopped dead. The shot was followed immediately by a scream from Mike, and she felt her blood run cold.

She had tried hard to recall the route she had run when she split up with Mike. She reckoned that she had headed deeper into the brewery. That meant that she needed to head in the direction of Mike's voice to get out again. She had been moving carefully towards that area but when the shot rang out, she froze. Packham shouted again.

'I've just shot your friend, Lucy. You should have shown yourself when I told you!'

Lucy felt sick.

'Don't worry – I only shot him in the leg!' Packham shouted. 'He doesn't *have* to die. But if you don't show yourself, I'll let him bleed to death.'

Lucy was terrified of what might happen if she surrendered to Packham. But could she really let her friend slowly bleed to death?

'Nobody needs to die, Lucy,' cried Packham. 'I'll just tie you and your friends up while I escape. But if Mike dies, it will be on your conscience forever!'

Lucy didn't know if Packham was lying about not killing them.

Maybe it was true, and he might not want the death of children on his hands. Maybe he really would just tie them and make his getaway. Or maybe he would shoot her too, once she surrendered.

'He's losing blood, Lucy!' called Packham. 'If you want me to stem the flow, time's running out!'

Lucy bit her lip, desperately torn between her choices. Then she steeled her nerves.

'All right!' she shouted. 'I'm coming in. Please – save him!'

Wilson moved soundlessly through the vathouse. He went to the back of the first of the huge steel vats, then continued moving silently as he looked for a stairway that would take him up onto the catwalks.

His plan was to outflank Packham, so that he could approach him unseen from the rear.

As Wilson had entered the vathouse through the open door he had heard Packham ordering Lucy to kneel on the catwalk beside Mike, with her hands on her head. It was brave of Lucy to give herself up, Wilson thought, but there was no guarantee that Packham would keep his word, and he might still kill both of them.

For now, though, Packham was distracted as he began to question Lucy and Mike, and Wilson knew that he had to act while he had the chance. It was frightening to think that everything depended on him, but his anger still drove him and he moved on quickly. Up ahead was a stairway that led towards the catwalks at the top of the gleaming steel vats.

Wilson took a deep breath, grabbed the handrail and began ascending.

* * *

Packham's face was tight with anger as he stared at Mike and Lucy. Mike tried to hold back his fear. Thinking clearly could save his life here, and he had to give himself and Lucy every chance. He felt sickened that she had fallen for Packham's trickery, even though he was glad that the gangster hadn't actually shot him – which he had sworn to do if Mike had called out a warning. Instead Packham had simply fired a shot into the air and twisted Mike's arm at the same time, so that he screamed. The shot-and-bleeding-to-death lie had been clever enough to fool Lucy, however, and now they both knelt at Packham's feet, their hands on their heads.

'I've seen your face before,' said Packham accusingly. 'What's your full name?'

'Mike Farrelly.'

'From where?'

Mike figured that the longer he could drag out the questions and answers the more time it would give Wilson to arrive back with the police.

'We came from Dublin originally, but my family moved to Canada when I was, let me see, about five...'

'I didn't ask for the family history!' snapped Packham. 'Where do you live now?!'

'In the grounds of The Grove School in Lakefield. My Dad's the janitor.'

'What have you told him about all this?'

Mike hesitated.

'Don't lie!'

'I've…I've told him nothing.' Mike suspected that Packham wouldn't believe him if he claimed that Da knew about the boathouse killing. Da, like most parents, would simply have called the police. Better to tell the truth but try to drag things out, he thought.

'Why didn't you tell him?' asked Packham.

'Because I promised Lucy I'd keep her secret.'

Packham turned his aggressive stare to Lucy. 'And who have you told?'

'I told nobody on the reserve,' she answered.

'Who did you tell *off* the reserve?'

'Just…just Mike and Wilson. I swear, the three of us kept it to ourselves.'

'What the hell were you doing on my estate in the first place?' he demanded.

'I was…I was just walking the trail. When I heard voices I ran into the boathouse.'

'Sticking your damn nose in!'

'Look, we're sorry, OK?' said Mike.

'No you're not! You're only sorry you got caught.'

'Either way,' said Mike, trying to make his tone sound reasonable, 'there's no need for things to get worse. You can still tie us up and escape, like you said.'

'Can I now? Know what you can do?' Packham pointed his finger aggressively. 'You can shut your mouth!'

Mike swallowed hard and didn't respond, then Packham turned his attention again to Lucy.

'You've caused me a whole heap of trouble. And you're going to pay for it.'

'I didn't mean any harm. I was just curious about where the trail led.'

'Big mistake! Redskins should stick to their reserves, not trespass on white men's land!'

Mike knew that would rile Lucy but he hoped she wouldn't argue back and make Packham even angrier. But Lucy was smart. She said nothing.

'Ever hear the old saying about curiosity? And what it did to the cat?' demanded Packham.

'Yes,' answered Lucy.

'Good. 'Cause tonight you'll see it in action.'

Packham gave a humourless smile, and Mike felt a shiver run up his spine.

Wilson reached the top of the stairway and stepped out onto the catwalk. He could hear Packham's voice as he threatened Mike and Lucy round the far side of the row of vats. Wilson had been moving as fast as he could while still remaining quiet, but now he paused. His anger had driven him this far, but knowing that he was about to face Packham, he felt a surge of fear.

He hesitated, trying to work up his courage. He breathed deeply, hoping to calm himself, but he knew he had to move on. If he waited any longer, he would lose his nerve. He thought of how his friends needed him, then he took a final breath and moved stealthily forward.

Lucy made sure to show her fear. It wasn't hard, as Packham's words really *were* frightening. But she deliberately tried to look as terrified as possible, reasoning that the more scared she looked, the less Packham would think of her as a threat.

It was obvious that he looked down on the Ojibwe, and a man like Packham would always think himself superior to a young girl. *Good*, Lucy thought, for once prejudice could actually work in her favour.

She had been furious when she realised that he had tricked her about Mike bleeding to death. But she had adapted to the new situation and followed Packham's order to kneel without giving away her one advantage – her hidden Bowie knife.

Although it wasn't as lethal as a gun, Lucy had the knife sheathed in a pocket inside her buckskin jacket. Of course, having a knife was one thing, getting access to it while being held at gun point was another matter. But even if she did get to it, would she be able to wield it faster than Packham could shoot with the pistol? And when it came to it, would she be able to stab another human being?

'Did you really think I'd tie you up and flee?' asked Packham now with a sneer. 'Leave behind my family, my brewery, the business I spent years building up? And all because a few brats couldn't mind their own business?'

Lucy swallowed hard. He had lied – he wasn't going to let them live. She gradually slid her hands from the top of her head to behind her head, anxious to get as near to the knife as she could without arousing suspicion.

'You should never have crossed Brent Packham. Nobody does that and gets away with it – nobody!'

Lucy slipped her hands a little further down, so that now they were just behind her neck. Although the man's words were frightening, his arrogance was so strong that he hadn't bothered to chastise Lucy for not keeping her hands on her head. But it would still be hard to get to the knife faster than he could shoot, and she needed something to distract him.

Even as she thought it, Lucy's heart suddenly soared. She could barely believe her eyes. Coming from around the corner of the vat was Wilson. He was out of sight to both Packham and Mike, but Lucy met his eye. Immediately he put a finger to his lips, and Lucy gave a barely perceptible nod.

Her mind was reeling. She had thought that Wilson was gone to get the police. Was this better or worse? If he had gone for the police, it might have been too late for her and Mike by the time they arrived. But Wilson was a small boy, and not used to fighting. Could he really take on Brent Packham, even with the element of surprise on his side? Lucy didn't know, but she prayed that somehow he could.

Mike racked his brain. He needed something to keep Packham engaged, and he said the first thing that came into his head. 'I've written to Moose about this!'

Packham looked taken aback. 'What?'

'Your son, Moose. I've sent him a letter, explaining about witnessing the killing.'

'What the hell were you doing writing to my son?'

Mike was struggling to come up with an answer, when he suddenly saw Wilson, creeping towards Packham from behind.

'Why did you write to Moose? Answer me!' repeated Packham.

Gobsmacked, Mike could see that Wilson had a glass bottle in one hand, but he had no idea what his friend's plan was. But the more he could distract Packham the better, so he decided to hold the man's attention with a challenging answer.

'I wanted him to know what kind of lousy father he had. That you're involved with murder. I wanted him to know that we were coming here tonight, so if anything happened us he'd know you'd stooped to murdering kids!' Mike was improvising wildly, but he had Packham's attention.

Wilson was only a few steps away now, and Mike held Packham's gaze. 'If you kill us tonight you'll never be able to look your son in the eye.'

Packham looked furious and cocked the pistol.

'Packham!' cried Wilson.

Packham swung round in shock, and Wilson threw the contents of the glass bottle into his eyes.

Mike was struck by the horrible smell of ammonia. Packham screamed as the ammonia struck him, and he fell back. Mike realised that he was only partially blinded, however, because even as he stumbled backwards Packham got off a shot.

The bullet barely missed Wilson and ricocheted off the metal vat. As Mike and Lucy staggered to their feet, Packham was clawing at his eyes with one hand but trying to aim the gun at Wilson with the other.

Wilson had dropped the glass bottle when diving aside to avoid the first shot. Now he was defenceless as Packham pointed the gun again. But before he could get a shot off Lucy leaped forward, and Mike saw a flash of steel. With a yell, she stabbed Packham in the ribs with her knife.

Packham screamed in pain and fury. He swung around and blindly fired two shots in quick succession. Both shots went astray, but Lucy had jumped backwards, and she lost her balance and fell. The knife slipped from her grip, and Mike dived to catch it, but it clattered along the metal catwalk and fell over the side. It banged off the side of the vat on the way down, then it hit the floor far below.

Mike swung around, and saw, to his horror, that Packham was

rubbing his eyes again and swivelling the gun. Blood was flowing from the wound in his side, but he was bringing the weapon to bear in the direction of Mike and Lucy.

Mike rolled away as a shot rang out. He felt the bullet whizzing by his ear, then suddenly there was another cry of rage from Packham. Wilson had hit him on the head with a metal spanner that had been hanging on the wall.

Dazed and half-blinded, Packham still kept hold of the gun. As Wilson hit him again, he lurched forward, heading straight for Mike. Mike realised he could easily get thrown over the low rail of the catwalk. Packham was big and strong, and despite the blow to the head and the stab wound, Mike feared that he could still overpower him. In desperation Mike tried a move he had seen in wrestling.

He allowed himself to fall back while kicking upwards with both legs. As Packham bore down on him at high speed, Mike's feet connected with Packham's stomach. The man's momentum carried him sailing over Mike's head.

There was a prolonged scream, followed by a heavy thud, and Mike realised that Packham had gone over the low railing on the catwalk and fallen to the vathouse floor.

One part of him was horrified, but his survival instincts overcame his revulsion. 'Quick,' he said, 'we need to get the gun first!'

Mike sprinted to the stairway and descended at speed, Lucy and Wilson just behind him. He could see that Packham lay unmoving on the ground, but he was taking no chances, and he ran to where the gun lay, several yards nearer the vathouse door.

Mike picked up the gun and approached gingerly. Now that he was nearer he could see that Packham had fallen awkwardly, and that his neck and head were at a strange angle.

'Oh my God!' said Wilson, 'I think he's broken his neck!'

'I'll check for a pulse,' said Lucy.

'Careful!' cried Mike. 'He might be faking.'

'I don't think he is,' said Lucy, her voice shaky, 'I think he's dead. Point the gun at him while I check.'

Mike drew closer, and he gripped the gun in both hands, aiming at Packham's heart.

The blood from the stab wound was pooling on the floor, and Mike suspected that Lucy might be right.

She dropped to her knees and placed a finger on Packham's neck for a few moments. Then she looked up at the boys and shook her head.

Mike felt a weird mixture of terror and relief. 'Mother of God,' he said, 'we've killed a man!'

CHAPTER THIRTY

Wilson felt the night air cooling the sweat on his brow as a breeze blew in off the Otonabee River, several blocks from Maple Brewery. The river glistened magically under a full moon, but Wilson had no appreciation for its beauty tonight.

They had sprinted out of the brewery, anxious to get away before Packham's men came. It was only when they had put a good distance between themselves and the scene of the killing that they had paused to catch their breath on the darkened river bank.

Wilson had just assumed that they would notify the police, and now he was shocked to find that Mike and Lucy didn't agree.

'We can't do this,' he said, 'we just can't!'

'You're not thinking straight, Will,' answered Lucy. 'What we can't do is go to the police. It was one thing to go with evidence of murder. It would be completely different telling them we killed someone.'

'But it was self-defence,' said Wilson.

'We know that. But they might see a man who'd been stabbed, beaten on the head and had his neck broken. We could end up in all sorts of trouble.'

'Surely the police can't convict us of anything?'

'Why take the chance?' asked Mike. 'And anyway, it's not just about us being convicted. There's other stuff.'

'Like what?'

'Your dad is an important businessman. How do you think it would look if his son was linked to a gangster? Linked to his killing?'

Wilson hadn't considered that and he was taken aback.

'And there's Lucy to consider,' added Mike. 'Indians don't get a fair deal in most things. Who knows how they'd use it against the Ojibwe if she's accused of killing a white man?'

'I hadn't thought of that,' conceded Wilson. 'But even so...'

'There's my da too,' said Mike. 'He and my ma were really lucky to find a school where they both have jobs. If there's a big scandal, they could be let go.'

'And there's another danger,' said Lucy. 'Even if the law cleared us, what about Packham's gangster friends? They could come after us and kill us. We can't live looking over our shoulders all the time. He got what he deserved, Will, we shouldn't have to suffer for it.'

Wilson realised that his friends had thought things out far more than he had. He reflected for a moment more, then nodded. 'OK,' he said softly.

"OK' isn't enough,' said Lucy. 'We can't talk to anyone about what's happened. Not now, not ever. We need to swear, that none of us will ever tell.'

'The Bible is against swearing,' said Wilson. As soon as he said it, he realised that it sounded petty compared to the matters of life and death they had encountered.

'For God's sake, Will,' said Mike. 'The Bible is against murder – and he'd have murdered us!'

Wilson raised his hands in surrender. 'You're right,' he said. 'I'm sorry, I should have seen these problems myself.'

'So you'll swear?' asked Mike.

Wilson looked at him, then nodded. 'Yes, I will.'

'It should be a solemn oath,' suggested Lucy, 'that we never tell another person as long as we live.'

'Agreed,' answered Mike, raising his hand. 'I give my solemn oath that I'll never tell.'

Lucy raised her hand. 'I give my solemn oath that I'll never tell.'

There was a pause as his two friends looked at him, then Wilson raised his hand. 'I give my solemn oath that I'll never tell. Amen.'

'Amen,' said the others.

CHAPTER THIRTY-ONE

Lucy stared at the flames, then slowly gazed upwards as the smoke billowed against the blue of the summer sky. She had lit the fire on a remote stretch of shoreline at Clear Lake, and now she stood, unmoving, and looked north towards the wild expanses of the Kawartha Highlands.

It was three days since the death of Brent Packham, and no questions had been asked of her, or of Mike or Wilson. On the night of the killing they had walked all the way home to Lakefield from Peterborough. The full moon had lit their way, and they had made sure to remain hidden whenever a motor vehicle had approached along the road. All of them had managed to slip back into their beds before dawn without being caught.

She reckoned by now that the police were unlikely ever to discover what had happened in Maple Brewery. They would probably assume that Packham had met his death at the hands of a rival, and eventually their enquiries would meet a dead end and peter out.

She had joined Mike and Wilson yesterday for a last gathering of the G Club. Wilson's father was coming to collect him today, and was taking him south for the rest of the summer. It meant that Mike would no longer be able to borrow the sailing skiffs from the school, and would revert to seeing his local friends in the mornings. Deep down, Lucy had known that the G Club couldn't last, yet when she said her farewells to the boys yesterday, she had tears in her eyes.

Now she looked up at the billowing smoke and thought of life and death. Brent Packham was being buried this morning in Peterborough, and Lucy had lit the fire to mark the passing of his spirit. He had been an evil man, but still a human being, and so she had prayed for his eternal soul. But now it was time to move on in her own life. She still had the rest of the summer in which to produce enough quality art to try to win the scholarship.

Her art materials were in her berthed canoe, and she planned to travel across the lake this morning and sketch the view northwards towards the Kawartha Highlands.

She watched the smoke for a moment more, then she reached down to her pitcher of water and doused the fire. She felt a sense of finality as the flames died, and she turned away and walked to the canoe, untied the mooring line and climbed in. Then she pushed off, picked up her paddle and headed north across the sunlit lake.

The atmosphere was awkward in the Farrellys' parlour, and Mike wasn't sure who was to blame.

When the boys had been together, or with Lucy, they had been easy in each other's company, despite their differences. Now, however, as Mike and Wilson sat in the parlour with Mr Taggart and the Farrellys, the atmosphere felt polite but strained. The Taggarts had called in before they departed on their delayed family holiday, and thanked Ma and Da for their hospitality to Wilson. But Ma had seemed slightly thrown when Mr Taggart had declined her offer of tea, and Da had spoken in the deferential tone that he used when talking to people that he regarded as his social superiors.

Mr Taggart, for his part, had been meticulously courteous to Ma and Da. But Mike felt that while he was sincere, his thank-yous felt like those a powerful employer might offer to a dutiful worker.

So the class difference seemed to affect all the adults, and Mike was also aware of his father's attitude to the Taggarts being Protestants. Was Wilson's father affected by this too, and was that why he had declined the offer of tea, and smiled pleasantly but without much warmth? If so, Mike thought it was sad all round. Why did adults have to be so complicated, he wondered, why couldn't they just accept each other the way he and Wilson had?

As though he were reading Mike's mind, Wilson gave a smile of real affection and held out his hand. 'Thanks for a great couple of weeks, Mike,' he said.

Mike shook his hand firmly and smiled back. 'It was good having you around.'

Wilson held his grip and spoke quietly. 'I won't forget this summer.'

'I won't either,' said Mike.

They both knew that Brent Packham was being buried in Peterborough today. Mike had overheard his parents discussing a rumour that Packham had been murdered by gangsters from the USA. It seemed that they had gotten away with the events in Maple Brewery.

He still wished that nobody had died. But Brent Packham had been an evil man, and Mike was satisfied that they had acted in self defence at the brewery. And with all that had happened, Moose would be unlikely to focus on the minor fight in the dormitory, so Mike felt that his parents' jobs were secure.

'Right, well, we'd better make for our train,' said Mr Taggart.

'OK, Dad,' answered Wilson, but he continued his handshake with Mike for one more moment before letting go.

The adults all said their goodbyes, then Mr Taggart lead the way through the parlour door.

''Bye, Mike,' said Wilson.

''Bye, Will.'

Wilson gave him a final wink, and Mike raised his hand in farewell, as his friend walked through the door.

A huge plume of thick, black smoke spouted from the funnel of the train as it jerked into motion. Steam whistled out of the side of the engine, and the carriages shuddered as the locomotive began to move out of Lakefield station.

Wilson sat opposite his father, their seats chosen on the right hand side of the carriage to afford a view of the Otonabee River as they travelled to Peterborough. Wilson's emotions were mixed, although he made sure to hide the fact from his father. On the one hand it was good to be reunited with him, and he looked forward to their train journey back to Toronto, and then onwards to a luxury resort in southern Ontario.

Another part of Wilson felt wistful, however. He had never felt more alive than when he was with Lucy and Mike, and apart from the terrifying final conflict with Brent Packham, it had been a great summer. But now that was all over. He had learnt a lot about art and Ojibwe life from Lucy. Perhaps more importantly, he had learnt from Mike to be braver, and to believe in himself. Before this summer he wouldn't have had the nerve to stand up to somone like Moose Packham, but now he had decided that he would never again live his life being fearful.

It helped that Moose wouldn't be returning to the school – Mrs Packham was moving back to live near her family in Detroit – but even if he had remained it wouldn't have mattered. Wilson would never let himself think like a victim in future, and, for that, he had Mike and Lucy to thank.

He was scheduled to return to school in September, but he knew that things wouldn't be the same. He hoped to see Mike and Lucy again, but the circumstances that had allowed them to spend so much time together wouldn't be repeated. Much as he treasured the fun that they had had, he knew in his heart that the

G Club had been for one summer only. But what a summer, he thought, what a summer!

'Penny for your thoughts, Wilson?' said his father.

'Just…thinking about the holidays,' he answered. He smiled at his father. Then he settled back in his seat and looked out the window as the train picked up speed and left Lakefield behind.

CHAPTER THIRTY-TWO

Ciara sat unmoving on the bench in the marsh. The sun was beating down, and the remains of her picnic were in the open lunch box by her side, but she could hardly remember having eaten. She had just finished Granddad's manuscript and had lost track of time. The life or death struggle that Granddad and his friends had with Brent Packham had engrossed her, and she felt she had relived the ordeal that the three children had been through.

She looked at her watch and realised that she should get back to the house before Dad began wondering what was keeping her. She gathered up her belongings, her mind still racing from the events of 1928. She could understand now why Granddad had kept his sworn promise to remain silent. There had been good reasons to prevent anyone knowing the role they had played in Packham's death.

Not that Ciara felt Granddad or his friends had anything of which to be ashamed. In fact she thought that the three of them had been really brave. Brave and loyal.

Ciara wondered again what she would have done if she had been alive back then. But it was impossible to guess how she would have behaved in such a different time. She felt that she had inherited some of Granddad's characteristics, though, so she liked to think that she would have been as courageous as he had been.

Whatever about what she might have done back in 1928, she felt no regrets now about the death of Packham. She hoped sincerely that Granddad had never felt any qualms either about the part he played in taking the gangster's life – not when it was so clearly in self-defence. But it was really strange to think that if Packham had succeeded, Granddad would have died as a twelve-year-old boy. In which case Dad would never have been born, and would never have come to Dublin and met Mam. It was weird to realise that she wouldn't exist today if things had gone differently back in Maple Brewery on that fateful night.

She rose from the bench, thinking that life was strange and unpredictable and precious. Most of all, she was simply glad that Granddad had lived to tell his tale – eventually. As she carefully placed the manuscript back in its envelope and put it in her rucksack, she felt proud that he had chosen her to be the first person to read his story.

She took one last look around the marsh where the members of the G Club had plotted, painted and told riddles.

'Good on you, Granddad,' she said softly, then she hoisted the rucksack onto her back and started for home.

EPILOGUE

Wilson withstood pressure from his father to enter the steel business and instead followed his dream of becoming a pilot. He served in the Canadian Air Force in the Second World War until he was invalided out after receiving serious injuries on a bombing raid over Germany. He convalesced for almost a year at his ancestral home near Kilrea in County Derry, and after the war he founded his own aviation company and settled in Vancouver.

Despite encouragement from Wilson over the years, Mr Taggart never remarried, instead channelling most of his energy into his foundry business. He ended his career as one of the biggest steel manufacturers in Canada but never fully accepted Wilson's decision not to enter the family firm.

Lucy won her scholarship and went on to become a successful artist, based in Toronto. She often came back to visit her mother and relatives, and was proud of her Ojibwe heritage. But after leaving home, she never lived again on a reserve, choosing instead to make her life in Toronto.

Lucy's mother continued her work as a herbalist and healer on the Otonabee Reserve, and remarried the same year that Lucy graduated from art college.

Moose Packham drifted into a life of crime, on the family's

return to Detroit. He served numerous sentences in prison, and died in jail of a heart attack at the age of fifty.

Hannah and Thomas Farrelly remained for several years as nurse and janitor at The Grove before becoming the matron and janitor at a school in Peterborough, near to where their married daughter Edith lived.

Mike and his brother Patrick also served in the Second World War, Mike as a fighter pilot and Patrick as an officer in the Canadian army. Patrick was killed at Dieppe, but Mike came through unscathed. He worked as an English teacher and later lectured at Trent University. He married and had one son, Dave, who went to college in Ireland, where he settled and raised a family in Blackrock, County Dublin.

Despite the close secret friendship that they had known, Mike, Lucy and Wilson went their separate ways, partly because their parents wouldn't have approved of their friendship, and partly because they moved in very different worlds once their summer adventures ended. But they never forgot the bond that they once had, never betrayed the secret oath that they swore, and never, for the rest of their days, forgot the special summer of 1928.

HISTORICAL NOTE

All of the historical events described in the story actually took place. For plot purposes I've located Lucy's home at the fictitious Otonabee Reserve on the shores of Lake Katchewanooka and brought back slightly the date of the summer holidays in The Grove School.

The families of Mike, Lucy and Wilson are figments of my imagination, but The Grove School was a real place that still operates today from the same location. Renamed as Lakefield College, it is now co-educational, and remains one of the foremost schools in Canada having, as a patron, Prince Andrew, who is a former pupil.

Curve Lake Reserve is also an actual place and officially became a reserve in 1837. The brass band that features in the story is also real, and Ojibwe musicians played in the Peterborough County of Ontario in the 1920s.

Elsie Knott from Curve Lake became the first woman chief in Canada in 1954, and members of the Ojibwe tribe finally got full voting rights as Canadian citizens in 1960.

The Trent Severn waterway, linking Lake Huron with Lake Ontario, passes through Lakefield as described, and the lift lock at Peterborough is still the highest hydraulic lock in the world.

The bridge at Young's Point from which Mike and Wilson

jumped still exists – although jumping from it nowadays is not encouraged.

Maple Brewery is fictitious, but the train stations in Peterborough and Lakefield were as described. The rail line on which Mike, Lucy and Wilson travelled between Lakefield and Peterborough was closed in 1989, and the route is now a greenway for walkers and cyclists.

Brian Gallagher
Dublin 2015